Air War Iraq

Operation IRAQI FREEDOM

By Lou Drendel

squadron/signal publications

(Previous Page) A Fairchild Republic A-10A Thunderbolt II (nicknamed the 'Warthog') of the 332nd Air Expeditionary Group (AEG) takes off on an early morning mission on 29 March 2003. This Group was based at Al Jaber Air Base (AB), Kuwait during Operation IRAQI FREEDOM. (USAF by SRA JoAnn S. Makinano)

(Front Cover) The object of Operation IRAQI FREEDOM was to remove the regime of Saddam Hussein and that meant removing Saddam himself. 'Leadership' targets were understood to mean Saddam or his closest associates, and the weapon of choice was airpower.

Introduction

"Iraq continues to flaunt its hostility toward America and to support terror. The Iraqi regime has plotted to develop anthrax, and nerve gas, and nuclear weapons for over a decade. This is a regime that has already used poison gas to murder thousands of its own citizens – leaving the bodies of mothers huddled over their dead children. This is a regime that agreed to international inspections – then kicked out the inspectors. This is a regime that has something to hide from the civilized world." – President George W. Bush, State of the Union Address to Congress, 29 January 2002.

Iraq was just one of the three 'Axis of Evil' states named by the President in this speech. Bush's catalog of Iraqi transgressions was far more detailed and extensive than that of Iran and North Korea, the other two nation states comprising this axis.

In January of 2002, the United States had already achieved a significant victory over terrorism. Operation ENDURING FREEDOM, begun on 7 October 2001, scored a quick and decisive defeat of the terrorist-sponsoring Taliban regime of Afghanistan. The al-Qaeda terrorist organization – hosted by the Taliban and responsible for the attacks of 11 September 2001 – was decimated and on the run. Although the war in Afghanistan would continue until al-Qaeda and their leaders were brought to justice, the President made it clear that the war on terror would not end with victory in Afghanistan or the death of al-Qaeda. He was dedicated to defeating terrorism throughout the world and Iraq was at the top of the list of states that the US would bring to justice. It was just a matter of time until the Iraqi regime was engaged.

The Iraq of President Saddam Hussein was the model of a rogue nation, an outlaw state that attacked its neighbors and governed its people by terror. It had fought an eight-year war with Iran in the 1980s, which ended inconclusively after millions of deaths on both sides. It had invaded and occupied Kuwait in 1990, only to be ejected in 1991 by a US-led coalition of nations. Although this defeat was humiliatingly decisive and extremely costly, Saddam Hussein continued to defy the international community by terrorizing his citizenry and developing weapons of mass destruction.

The Clinton Administration and a long list of appeasing nations imposed ineffective and unenforced sanctions throughout the 1990s. The failure to provide consequences for Iraq's continued flaunting of United Nations resolutions encouraged the Hussein regime to push harder at the limits imposed by the 1991 Gulf War settlements.

The 11 September 2001 terrorist attacks on the US galvanized the Bush Administration. In his 2002 State of the Union speech, President Bush declared worldwide war on terrorism and terrorists. While most of the country and many political leaders were focused on retribution for

Iraqi dictator Saddam Hussein addresses his people and the world from Baghdad. Saddam's three decades-plus reign of terror came to a cataclysmic end within a few weeks of Operation IRAQI FREEDOM's beginning on 20 March 2003.

ISBN 0-89747-465-1

If you have any photographs of aircraft, armor, soldiers or ships of any nation, particularly wartime snapshots, why not share them with us and help make Squadron/Signal's books all the more interesting and complete in the future. Any photograph sent to us will be copied and the original returned. The donor will be fully credited for any photos used. Please send them to:

Squadron/Signal Publications, Inc.
1115 Crowley Drive
Carrollton, TX 75011-5010

Если у вас есть фотографии самолётов, вооружения, солдат или кораблей любой страны, особенно, снимки времён войны, поделитесь с нами и помогите сделать новые книги издательства Эскадрон/Сигнал ещё интереснее. Мы переснимем ваши фотографии и вернём оригиналы. Имена приславших снимки будут сопровождать все опубликованные фотографии. Пожалуйста, присылайте фотографии по адресу:

Squadron/Signal Publications, Inc.
1115 Crowley Drive
Carrollton, TX 75011-5010

軍用機、装甲車両、兵士、軍艦などの写真を 所持しておられる方はいらっしゃいませんか？どの国のものでも結構です。作戦中に撮影されたものが特に良いのです。Squadron/Signal社の出版する刊行物において、このような写真は内容を一層充実し、興味深くすること ができます。当方にお送り頂いた写真は、複写の後お返しいたします。出版物中に写真を使用した場合は、必ず提供者のお名前を明記させて頂きます。お写真は下記にご送付ください。

Squadron/Signal Publications, Inc.
1115 Crowley Drive
Carrollton, TX 75011-5010

these attacks, the Bush Administration saw the larger picture and the likelihood of more attacks if the United States remained as passive as it had been in the preceding decade.

"Thousands of dangerous killers, schooled in the methods of murder, often supported by outlaw regimes, are now spread throughout the world like ticking time bombs, set to go off without warning." He vowed that the United States will be *"steadfast, and patient, and persistent."* – President Bush, State of the Union Address, 29 January 2002.

Operation ENDURING FREEDOM was the first campaign in the war on terror and Operation IRAQI FREEDOM would be the second.

Combat Operations

It may be true that the generals always fight the last war; however, it was the retired generals that fought the last war in this conflict. Throughout the 2003 Iraq war, the various news networks hired a variety of retired military men to analyze and comment on current operations. Some high-ranking DESERT STORM generals criticized the war's conduct. They couldn't have been more wrong, but their analysis was based on their experience and information that was a decade out of date.

Operation IRAQI FREEDOM commanders mostly kept their own counsel and let the results of the campaign speak for them. General Tommy Franks – Commander-in-Chief of US Central Command (CENTCOM) – rarely appeared at the daily CENTCOM press briefings in Doha, Qatar. When he did, Franks was steadfast in the assertion that the war's outcome was never in doubt. When the generals did comment, their comments were to-the-point. Some examples:

"...I find it interesting when folks say we're softening them [The Republican Guard] *up. We're not softening them up. We're killing them."* – LGen T. Michael Moseley, Combined Forces Air Component Commander. *"If they fly, they die. It's as simple as that."* – BGen

Vincent Brooks, CENTCOM spokesman, on the Iraqi Air Force. *"The forces on this battlefield are the most capable I've ever seen, whether it's by way of technology or training or motivation. Our resolve is great. The morale is good. And there is no doubt about the outcome."* – Gen Tommy Franks, CENTCOM Commander-in-Chief.

At 0534 local time in Baghdad on 20 March 2003, US and United Kingdom (UK) forces began operations against Iraq. The initial strikes consisted of 40 cruise missiles and strikes led by two F-117s from the 8th Fighter Squadron, supported by Navy EA-6B Prowlers and other aircraft. These attacks came shortly after the expiration of the 48 hour deadline President Bush had given Iraqi President Saddam Hussein to leave Iraq. This attack was aimed directly at Hussein and signaled a major change in US policy in the conduct of war.

"There can be no such thing as fellowship with tyrants, nothing but bitter feud is possible: and it is not repugnant to nature to despoil, if you can, those whom it is a virtue to kill; nay, this pestilent and godless brood should be utterly banished from human society. For, as we amputate a limb in which the blood and the vital spirit have ceased to circulate, because it injures the rest of the body, so monsters, who under human guise, conceal the cruelty and ferocity of a wild beast, should be severed from the common body of humanity." – Cicero's De Officiis

The long-standing proscription against assassination of enemy political leaders was officially ended by this initial strike, which had been aimed at *"an enemy leadership target"* understood to be Saddam Hussein and his senior leaders. Although this strike failed to get Saddam, it was significant for more than the aforementioned policy change. The fact that intelligence considered to be reliable had provided the targeting information also signaled a highly different way of war.

Allied special forces had infiltrated Iraq long before the start of hostilities and had mapped the most important strategic targets for targeting planners. These included leadership, command and control, and military targets. They continued to provide targeting information throughout the aerial campaign, including a second direct attempt at Saddam. They were highly active in Northern Iraq, where they worked with Kurdish forces to defeat the Iraqi army. They also paved the way for the insertion, via air drop, of the 173rd Airborne Brigade.

A great deal of publicity has been given to the technological advances that have made the United States the most powerful military nation in history. Less publicized, but militarily as significant, are the capabilities of the human elements of US Special Operations Command (USSOCOM). Their ability to bond with the indigenous population and conduct effective military operations was demonstrated dramatically in Afghanistan, when less than 1000 special operations troops coordinated attacks that defeated the Taliban in less time than it took to get regular ground forces into the theater. Their contribution to the victory in Iraq was no less important.

Airpower led the ground attack in Operation DESERT STORM in 1991 and was used more extensively in support of the ground war in Operation IRAQI FREEDOM. This was primarily because the 2003 ground war began immediately, catching the Iraqi military completely off-guard and unprepared. The 3rd Infantry Division and the 1st Marine Division raced northward towards Baghdad, while British forces secured Basra and the southern sections of Iraq. Airpower's ability to conduct precision strikes became even more effective at providing Close Air Support (CAS).

During DESERT STORM, roughly ten percent of the munitions used were Precision-Guided Munitions (PGMs), or 'smart bombs.' During Operation IRAQI FREEDOM, that number went up to 80 percent and the bombs were even smarter. PGMs used in 1991 were laser or electro-optical (television) guided, which were unable to see through clouds or the smoke of battle. Although these weapons were still in use and were effective when employed under ideal conditions, they were mostly supplanted by the Global Positioning System (GPS)-guided Joint Direct Attack Munitions (JDAMs). JDAMs were far more effective and far cheaper ($1,000,000 each for laser-guided bombs vs. $32,000 each for JDAMs). The Iraqi generals really did fight the last war when they burned oil-filled trenches to foil PGMs. Their attempts to jam GPS signals with Russian jammers came to naught when GPS-guided bombs destroyed the jammers!

The ground war began on Day One of the war, when Coalition infantry crossed into Iraq and headed for Basra and Baghdad. Selected leadership targets were struck within Baghdad and Basra. Command and control and artillery positions were attacked and destroyed in Western Iraq, where special forces had been operating and subsequently captured Iraqi airfields. On the war's second day (21 March), the full force of Coalition aerial might was brought to bear on leadership targets within Baghdad. Often referred to as *"Shock and Awe,"* this series of attacks was made exclusively with PGMs in an attempt to limit collateral damage. These attacks would continue throughout the conflict, as intelligence sources pinpointed Iraqi leadership targets.

Aircraft used in these attacks included B-52s, B-1s, B-2s, F-15Es, F-16s, F-14s, AV-8s, A-10s, F/A-18s, and F-117s. Attacks originated from as far away as Whiteman AFB, Missouri (B-2s, who flew 34-hour round-trip missions), the United Kingdom (B-52s), Diego Garcia in the Indian Ocean (B-52s, B-2s), as well as 30 different bases in the CENTCOM Area of Responsibility (AOR) and five aircraft carriers. A variety of Coalition ships launched over 1000 Tomahawk Land Attack Missiles (TLAMs) – cruise missiles – that also played a major role in the *"Shock and Awe"* campaign. Over 700 aircraft dropped 3000 PGMs on the campaign's first day.

The ground advance was slowed on the 5th and 6th days of the war (24-25 March) by an intense sandstorm, which even affected ships operating in the Persian Gulf (Arabian Gulf). Iraqi resistance was stiff at times, but the lack of effective command and control meant that most of the Iraqi defenders were either killed, captured, or simply took off their uniforms and fled. Many of the firefights were intense and resulted in US casualties, but their outcome was never in doubt. Elements of the 3rd Infantry Division, 101st Airborne Division, and 1st Marine Expeditionary Force reached Baghdad's outskirts on Day 15 (3 April).

The war to decapitate the Iraqi leadership recorded another apparent success on the night of 4-5 April. Coalition aircraft struck the residence of Ali Hassan al-Majid, Saddam Hussein's cousin, who was notorious for ordering Iraqi forces to use chemical weapons on Kurds in northern Iraq. Al-Majid was infamously known as 'Chemical Ali.' US forces originally believed that al-Majid was killed in the raid, but he escaped and was arrested by US troops on 21 August.

In a demonstration of how quickly coalition air assets are able to adjust to *"targets of opportunity,"* a USAF B-1B bomber was diverted from a mission in Western Iraq to attack a residence in Baghdad on the war's Day 19 (7 April). Following intelligence that Saddam Hussein and his two sons may have been attending a meeting in the al-Mansour section of Baghdad, the B-1 dropped JDAMs on the suspected meeting place of senior Iraqi regime leaders. The strike at 1400 hours Qatar time used four 2000 pound (907 KG) JDAMs. These included 'Version 3' JDAMs, also called 'bunker busters' for their deep penetrating capability. At least three buildings were destroyed in the attack, which left a huge smoking crater. Since this section of Baghdad was not yet under Coalition control, it was not possible to do an on-site bomb damage assessment to determine whether Hussein or his sons were present. In fact, they left the residence just before the raid.

As the third week of the war drew to a close, units of the 1st Marine Division – moving through Baghdad from the east – linked up with the US 3rd Infantry Division (Mechanized), holding positions in the central city. In a scene transmitted live throughout the world, US troops assisted Iraqi citizens in toppling a large statue of Saddam Hussein. If ever there was an image declaring the end of the Hussein Regime, this was it. Although the northern cities of Kirkuk, Mosul, and Tikrit remained in Iraqi Army control, it was only a matter of time until those cities also fell to Coalition forces.

Tikrit fell on Day 26 of the war (14 April). It was the last major city in Iraqi control and it was symbolically important as Saddam Hussein's home town. Also symbolically important was the manner in which it fell. It was reported to be defended by 2500 hard-core Republican Guard troops. After intense aerial bombardment, those troops abandoned their weapons, uniforms and positions, fleeing in a full-scale rout.

On 1 May 2003, President Bush sat in the starboard seat of an S-3B Viking when he landed aboard the aircraft carrier USS ABRAHAM LINCOLN (CVN-71) off California. Later that day, he announced the end of major combat operations in Iraq from LINCOLN's flight deck.

This United States Air Force (USAF) chart provides graphic evidence of the quantum advances in the effectiveness of airpower provided by precision guided munitions. CEP refers to Circular Error Probability. (USAF)

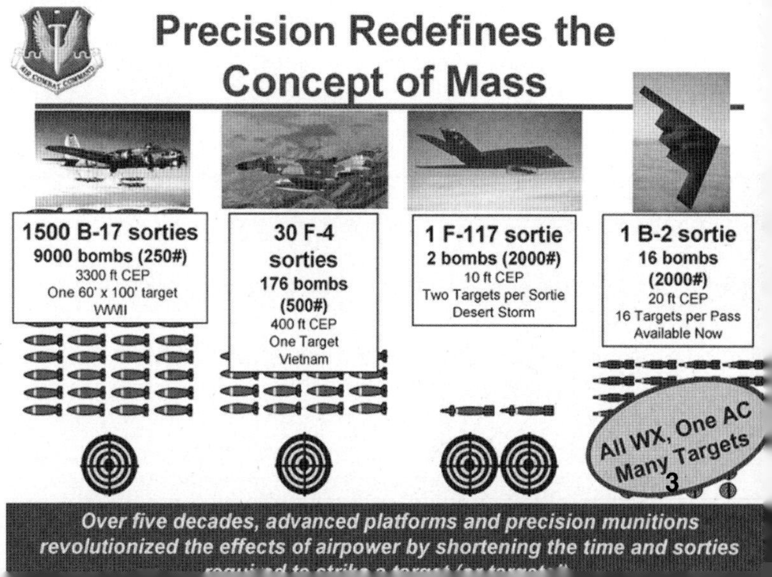

A Boeing B-52H Stratofortress of the 457th Air Expeditionary Wing (AEW) heads for Iraq. Six 2000 pound (907 KG) GBU-31 Joint Direct Attack Munitions (JDAMs) are mounted on the wing pylons. The B-52's maiden flight occurred in 1954 and Boeing completed 744 B-52s – including 102 B-52Hs – through 1962. The USAF has 94 B-52Hs remaining in service and they are projected to serve until 2045. No less than five generations of B-52 pilots will have flown the 'BUFF' (Big Ugly Fat Fella) before it is finally retired! (USAF)

B-52H *BOMBER BARONS* (61-6023) taxies out at RAF Fairford, England for another IRAQI FREEDOM mission. Under the black outline squadron insignia on the nose, it displays four mission symbols for AGM-86C/D Conventional Air Launched Cruise Missile (CALCM) launches. IRAQI FREEDOM was the first wartime use of the hard target CALCM. The Boeing AGM-86 is a turbofan-powered cruise missile with a range of 600 nautical miles (691 miles/1112 KM). It is 20 feet, nine inches (6.3 M) long, and weighs 3250 pounds (1474 KG) at launch. Block II CALCMs have Global Positioning System (GPS) guidance and hard target penetrating capability. This B-52H was reassigned from the 23rd Bomb Squadron (BS), 5th Bomb Wing (BW) at Minot Air Force Base (AFB), North Dakota to an Expeditionary Bomb Squadron (EBS) for IRAQI FREEDOM. (Stephen Drew via Andre Jans)

A 40th EBS B-52H pilot signals ready with a 'thumbs-up' prior to launching. B-52s carried a wide variety of weapons, including conventional Mk 80 series bombs, Laser Guided Bombs (LGBs), JDAMs, and ALCMs. The USAF deployed 28 B-52Hs during Operation IRAQI FREEDOM. They achieved a mission-capable rate of 76.7 percent. New York Police Department (NYPD) and Fire Department of New York (FDNY) emblems are painted under GOD BLESS AMERICA on the nose. Aft of the main nose art is the Bossier City Police Department insignia. (Bossier City, Louisiana is the nearest city to this B-52H's home base, Barksdale AFB.) (USAF by TSgt Richard Freeland)

A B-52H (60-0051), formerly of the 23rd BS at Minot AFB, departs RAF Fairford for an Operation IRAQI FREEDOM mission. The B-52 has an unrefueled range of 8800 miles (14,162 KM) and has flown some of the longest combat missions in history. (Stefan Buysse via Andre Jans)

(Right) A 40th EBS B-52H radar navigator runs a weapons targeting check during an IRAQI FREEDOM bombing mission on 30 March 2003. Operation IRAQI FREEDOM was the first wartime use by a B-52 of an LGB guided by the Rafael Litening II pod. This pod enabled the Stratofortress to guide their own LGBs, instead of relying on laser guidance from other aircraft or ground forces. Litening II pods were also carried into battle by some F-16C/D Fighting Falcons, A-10 Thunderbolt IIs, and F-15E Strike Eagles. (USAF by TSgt Richard Freeland)

(Lower Right) A Boeing KC-135 Stratotanker refuels a B-52H over the Indian Ocean on 24 March 2003. The KC-135 crew was from the 931st Air Refueling Group (ARG) from McConnell AFB, Kansas. They were assigned to the 405th Air Expeditionary Wing (AEW), deployed to Thumrait AB, Oman in support of Operations IRAQI FREEDOM in Iraq and ENDURING FREEDOM in Afghanistan. (USAF by SSgt Cherie A. Thurpoundy)

(Below) Capt Jason McNutt of the 40th EBS maneuvers his B-52 into position for a refueling from a Boeing KC-135 Stratotanker during an IRAQI FREEDOM bombing mission. All B-52s are equipped with an Electro-optical Viewing System (EVS) that uses Forward-Looking Infra-Red (FLIR) and high-resolution Low-Light level Television (LLTV) sensors to augment targeting, battle assessment, and flight safety. (USAF by TSgt Richard Freeland)

A B-52H (60-0051) departs RAF Fairford with GBU-31 JDAMs loaded on its external racks. The Joint Direct Attack Munition (JDAM) is a tail kit fitted to conventional Mk 80-series bombs to provide precision GPS guidance to the munition. JDAMs can be dropped from up to 15 miles (24 KM) from the target. The 1000 pound (454 KG) JDAM variant is designated the GBU-31 and the 2000 pound (907 KG) version is designated the GBU-32. JDAM variants for the Mk 80 250 pound (113 KG) and Mk 81 500 pound (227 KG) bombs are designated GBU-29 and GBU-30, respectively. Hard target penetrators being changed into low-cost JDAMs included the 2000 pound BLU-109 and 1000 pound BLU-110. (Stefan Buysse via Andre Jans)

SRA Nicolas Cox of the 509th Aircraft Maintenance Squadron (AMS) supervises the unloading of a GBU-31 JDAM from a Northrop Grumman B-2A Spirit at Whiteman AFB, Missouri. The Spirit was reloaded with a different weapon for another combat sortie. One of the armorers chalked SPECIAL DELIVERY on the JDAM. (USAF)

A Boeing North American B-1B Lancer (a.k.a. 'Bone') of the 405th AEW drops off the tanker en route to Iraq on 25 March 2003. The outer wing panels are fully extended at a 15° sweep angle for low-speed flight. They are swept aft up to 67.5° for high-speed flight. The USAF deployed 11 B-1Bs from the 28th BW at Ellsworth AFB, South Dakota for Operation IRAQI FREEDOM. (USAF by SSgt Cherie A. Thurpoundy)

A Northrop Grumman B-2A Spirit is en route to an 'undisclosed location' after completing a mission over Iraq. Operation IRAQI FREEDOM marked the first time that B-2s were forward-deployed. Previously, all missions began and ended at Whiteman AFB, although Diego Garcia in the Indian Ocean was used as an intermediate rest stop during Operation ENDURING FREEDOM. (USAF by SSgt Cherie A. Thurpoundy)

(Above) The B-2A SPIRIT OF KITTY HAWK (93-1086) taxies to parking at Whiteman AFB after an IRAQI FREEDOM mission. The Spirit's initial claim to fame was its low observable (stealth) capabilities, but its leading edge technology makes them so effective. (USAF by TSgt Michael R. Nixon)

A B-1B Lancer takes off from Andersen AFB, Guam on 14 March 2003. The 'Bones' were deployed from Dyess AFB, Texas to Andersen in support of the 7th AEW. This move allowed Lancers from Ellsworth AFB to head for Diego Garcia and Thumrait for Operation IRAQI FREEDOM. (USAF by A1C Joshua Strang)

(Below) Airmen secure 2000 pound JDAMs to a bomb trailer prior to loading them aboard B-1Bs at Thumrait AB, Oman on 21 March 2003. B-1s maintained a 79.4 percent mission-capable rate throughout the war. US aircraft dropped 6542 JDAMs during Operation IRAQI FREEDOM. (USAF by SSgt Jessica Kochman)

(Above) GHOST RIDER (61-007), a B-52H from Minot AFB, taxies out for an OPERATION IRAQI FREEDOM mission from RAF Fairford. It is armed with 2000 pound GBU-31 JDAMs. The small wheel forward of the main landing gear is the starboard outrigger wheel. B-52s have single outrigger wheels mounted in the outer wings to prevent the wingtips from striking the ground. (Stephen Drew via Andre Jans)

(Left) IRON Butterfly was a B-52H (60-0060) that launched its share of the 153 CALCMs expended during Operation IRAQI FREEDOM. The B-52H's gross takeoff weight is 488,000 pounds (221,357 KG). (USAF)

(Left) This B-52H (60-0047) returns to RAF Fairford after a mission over Iraq. Six CALCM silhouettes are painted within a box on the lower nose. Operation IRAQI FREEDOM marked the first time that B-1Bs, B-2As, and B-52Hs were used in the same strike package. That trio of bombers flew 505 sorties during IRAQI FREEDOM. (Stephen Drew via Andre Jans)

(Below) B-52H VICTORY THROUGH LOGISTICS (60-0026) taxies at Fairford for an OPERATION IRAQI FREEDOM mission. Its pilot displays a US flag through the cockpit window while the Stratofortress taxies to the active runway. (Stephen Drew via Andre Jans)

A B-1B is towed to parking after a mission. Lancers that participated in Operation IRAQI FREEDOM came from the 28th BW at Ellsworth AFB. They were reassigned to the 405th EBS (Composite) at Thumrait AB, Oman. (USAF by A1C Joshua Strang)

B-1Bs of the 28th BW return to Ellsworth AFB after Operation IRAQI FREEDOM. It was a 'Bone' that almost delivered the *coup de grace* to Saddam Hussein. It responded within minutes to the call for retargeting a leadership target in downtown Baghdad. Four JDAMs destroyed the buildings that Saddam and his sons were reported to be meeting; however, they had just left the premises before the raid.

(Below) B-1B JAGGED EDGE of the 37th BS taxies in at Ellsworth. Six B-1s and their crews returned to a crowd of family and friends welcoming them home. Lancers are cleared to deliver all sizes of JDAMs. B-1Bs were maintained at an 80 percent mission-capable rate during the war. 'Bones' flew 497 combat sorties supporting operations ENDURING FREEDOM and IRAQI FREEDOM and dropped 4.56 million pounds of munitions through 8 May 2003. (USAF by A1C Karah McNeill)

(Above) Capt Jennifer Wilson was the first female B-2 pilot to fly a combat mission. Wilson had previously flown the B-1B. Another B-2 first chalked up in Operation IRAQI FREEDOM was the delivery of Mk 82 'dumb' (unguided) bombs in combat. (USAF by TSgt Richard Freeland)

US CENTCOM – Air Forces

Air Order of Battle

Land Based Aircraft

Unit	Squadron	Location	Aircraft
	75 Sq [RAAF Tindal]		14 F/A-18s
	36 Sq [RAAF Richmond]		2 C-130Hs
	37 Sq [RAAF Richmond]		1 C-130Js
	92 Wing [RAAF Edinburgh]		2 P-3Cs
	157th Fighter Sq		15 F-16C/Ds
	190th Fighter Sq	**Kuwait**	A-10
	15th Reconnaissance Sq		RQ-1
	38th Rescue Sq		
	57th Rescue Sq		
	58th Rescue Sq		MH-60
	66th Rescue Sq		MH-60
	20th Special Operations Sq		MH-53M
	No. 216 Squadron [UK RAF]		1 L-1011 Tristar
	U/I Unit		3 UC-12Ms
	133rd Airlift Wing		
	139th Airlift Wing		
	22nd Air Refueling Wing		10 KC-135s
	100th Air Refueling Wing		
	element, 9th Reconnaissance Wing	**RAF Fairford**	- U-2S
	element 193rd Special Operations Wing		EC-130E
	33rd Fighter Wing		10 F-15s
	58th Fighter Sq		F-15s
	52nd Fighter Wing		
	23rd Fighter Sq	**Kuwait**	F-16CJs
	81st Fighter Sq	**Kuwait**	A-10s
	23rd Fighter Group		
	75th Fighter Sq		A-10s
	103rd Fighter Wing		
	111th Fighter Wing		
457th Air Expeditionary Group		**RAF Fairford**	
U/I Unit		**Jordan**	
401st Air Expeditionary Wing		**Souda Bay, Crete**	
	351st Air Refueling Sq		KC-135s
	U/I Sq, 319th Air Refueling Wing		KC-135s
409th Air Expeditionary Group		**Bourgas/Sarafovo, Bulgaria**	
	U/I Air Refueling Sq, 507 ARW		2 KC-10s
U/I Unit		**Constanta, Romania**	
39th Air and Space Expeditionary Wing		**Incirlik AB, Turkey**	
[NORTHERN WATCH]			
9th Air and Space Expeditionary Task Force			
363rd Air Expeditionary Wing		**Prince Sultan AB, Saudi Arabia**	
	390th Fighter Squadron (AEF 7)		F-15s
	14th Fighter Squadron (AEF 7)		18 F-16Js
	524th Fighter Sq (AEF 7)		18 F-16s
	457th Fighter Sq		6 F-16s
	363 Expeditionary Airborne Air Control Sq		6 E-3 AWACS
	U/I Air Control Sq		2 E-8 J-STARS
	38th Reconnaissance Sq (AEF 7)		4 RC-135s
	U/I Airlift Sq		
	VAQ-142		2 EA-6Bs
	99th Reconnaissance Sq (AEF 7)		2 U-2s
	U/I MEDEVAC Company		6 UH-60s
	No. 11 Squadron [UK RAF]		6 Tornado F.3s
	No. 25 Squadron [UK RAF]		Tornado F.3s
	No. 43 Squadron [UK RAF]		Tornado F.3s
	No. 111 Squadron [UK RAF]		4 Tornado F.3s
	element of 92nd Air Refueling Wing		12 KC-135s
	92nd Air Refueling Sq (AEF 7)		5 KC-135s

Unit	Squadron	Location	Aircraft
40th Air Expeditionary Wing		**Diego Garcia**	
	40th Bomb Squadron		B-52s
	20th Bomb Squadron (AEF 7)		10 B-52s
	462nd Air Expeditionary Group		12 KC-135Rs
386th Air Expeditionary Group		**Ali al Salem AB, Kuwait**	
	118th Fighter Sq		
	320th Exp Aeromedical Evac Sq		
	41st Electronic Combat Sq (AEF 7)		EC-130Hs
	71st Rescue Squadron		2 HC-130Ps
	No. 9 Squadron [UK RAF]		8 Tornado GR.4s
	No. 12 Squadron [UK RAF]		Tornado GR.4s
	No. 13 Squadron [UK RAF]		Tornado GR.4s
	No. 14 Squadron [UK RAF]		Tornado GR.4s
	No. 31 Squadron [UK RAF]		Tornado GR.4s
	No. 617 Squadron [UK RAF]		Tornado GR.4s
	U/I Unit		RC-12s
	U/I Unit		RQ-1Bs
332nd Air Expeditionary Group		**Al Jaber AB, Kuwait**	
	332nd Expd Air Sprt Ops Sqdn		
	332nd Expd Intel Flt		
	172nd Fighter Sq (AEF 7)		12 A-10s
	U/I Fighter Squadron		18 F-15Cs
	U/I unit		10 F-15Es
	22nd Fighter Squadron		8 F-16s
	189th Airlift Squadron		8 C-130s
	332nd Expd Rescue Sqdn		2 HH-60Gs
	U/I element of 552nd Air Control Wing		7 E-3 AWACS
355th Air Expeditionary Group		**Masirah AB, Oman**	
	U/I Unit		6 KC-135Rs
	U/I element of 911th Airlift Wing		8 C-130s
	4th Special Operations Squadron		6 AC-130Us
	8th Special Operations Squadron		MC-130Es
320th Air Expeditionary Wing		**Seeb IAP, Oman**	
	U/I Fighter Squadron		
	778 Exp Airlift Sq		C-130s
	189th Airlift Sq (AEF 7)		C-130s
405th Air Expeditionary Wing		**Thumrait AB, Oman**	
	405th Expeditionary Bomb Sq [Composite]		B-1Bs
	U/I Unit		4 E-3A AWACS
	U/I Unit		5 KC-135Rs
	U/I Unit		1 C-130s
	U/I element of 55th Wing		RC-135s
	No. 201 Squadron		1 Nimrod MR.2
	No. 206 Squadron		1 Nimrod MR.2
	element of 28th Bomb Wing		8 B-1Bs
	element of 34th Bomb Sq		B-1Bs
	element of 37th Bomb Sq		B-1Bs
379th Air Expeditionary Wing		**Al Udeid AB, Qatar**	
	U/I unit		F-16s
	379th Expeditionary Air Refueling Sqdn		4 KC-10s
	44th Expeditionary Air Refueling Sqdn		4 KC-10s
	340th Expeditionary Air Refueling Sqdn		2 KC-135Rs
	911th Air Refueling Sqdn		2 KC-135Rs
	U/I Unit of 434th Refueling Wing		2 KC-135Rs
	U/I element of 93rd Air Control Wing		2 E-8 J-STARS
	8th Fighter Squadron		4 F-117s
380th Air Expeditionary Wing		**Al Dhafra AB, UAE**	
	U/I element of 9th Reconnaissance Wing		2 U-2s
	11th Recon Sq		
	15th Recon Sq		RQ-4s
	12th Recon Sqdn		1 RQ-4
	763 Expeditionary Air Refueling Sq		4 KC-10s
	908 Expeditionary Air Refueling Sq		4 KC-10s

Sq – Squadron
RAAF – Royal Australian Air Force
UK RAF – United Kingdom Royal Air Force
U/I – Unidentified
AEF – Air Expeditionary Force
VAQ – US Navy Electronic Attack Squadron
MEDEVAC – Medical Evacuation
AWACS – Airborne Warning And Control System
J-STARS – Joint-Surveillance and Target Acquisition Radar System

Exp – Expeditionary
Sprt Ops Sqdn – Support Operations Squadron
Intel Flt – Intelligence Flight
UAE – United Arab Emirates

USAF weapons loaders prepare a B-52 weapons bay for loading of AGM-86C Conventional Air-Launched Cruise Missiles (CALCMs). Eight missiles are mounted onto a Multi-Purpose Launcher (MPL), which releases one CALCM at a time when the MPL rotates within the weapons bay. Stratofortresses launched 153 AGM-86C/D CALCMs against key Iraqi targets during the war. (USAF by SRA Christina M. Rumsey)

A Lockheed Martin F-16C Fighting Falcon 'Viper' pilot of the 410th AEW checks his Laser-Guided Bombs (LGBs) prior to a 21 March 2003 mission. Despite the rise in popularity of GPS-guided JDAMs, LGBs were used more often. The 500 pound (227 KG) GBU-12 was the most popular bomb in the war, with some 7114 being expended. (USAF by SSgt Samuel A. Park)

(Above) SSgt David Rohde, a B-2 Spirit crew chief applies another mission marking to the nose landing gear door after the 31 March 2003 mission. B-2s flew most missions from Whiteman AFB, Missouri, resulting in 34-hour mission times and multiple refuelings. The two-pilot crew alternates rest periods to accommodate these global missions. (USAF by A1C Nick Martin)

(Right) Armament personnel of the 332nd AEG load unguided ('dumb') bombs onto a Fairchild Republic A-10A Thunderbolt II (a.k.a. 'Warthog') prior to a 29 March 2003 mission. A-10s provided Close Air Support (CAS) from several locations, including the captured Iraqi airfield at Talil. (USAF by SRA JoAnn S. Makinano)

A 23rd FW A-10A is parked between missions under a temporary shelter. The 23rd FW traces its lineage to the American Volunteer Group 'Flying Tigers' of World War Two fame. They have proudly displayed their sharkmouth on its aircraft ever since they first adorned the P-40s of Claire Chennault's legendary volunteer unit The A-10 was literally designed around the 30MM General Electric GAU-8/A Avenger cannon in its nose. The seven-barreled GAU-8/A is 20 feet (6.1 M) long and weighs 4000 pounds (1814 KG). It fires a mix of Depleted Uranium (DU) and High Explosive (HE) shells, each nearly one foot (0.3 M) in length, at a rate of over 3900 rounds per minute. The gun's enormous force punches through even the latest reactive armor. (USAF)

This A-10A, from the 23rd FW at Pope AFB, North Carolina, sustained major combat damage on a CAS mission. Its pilot, call sign 'Killer Chick,' managed to return to base despite loss of hydraulics. A-10s operated in the environment for which they were designed, more than three decades before Operation IRAQI FREEDOM. Redundant systems and the pilot's titanium bathtub made it possible to take much punishment and keep flying. (USAF)

SRA Jay Labrum of the 124th Maintenance Squadron (MS) from the Idaho ANG, performs an operational check on an in-flight refueling receptacle on the nose of the A-10A. A1C Kyle Austin of the 43rd MS from Pope AFB monitors from the cockpit. (USAF by MSgt Stefan Alford)

Armament personnel of the 332nd AEW load 500 pound Mk 82 bombs on an A-10A prior to a 28 March 2003 mission from Talil AB, Iraq. Despite the much-publicized popularity of smart bombs, US aircraft dropped 5504 Mk 82s on Iraqi positions during Operation IRAQI FREEDOM. (USAF by SRA JoAnn S. Makinano)

Major Gary Wolf managed to nurse his Battle Creek 'Warthog' 150 miles (241 KM) back to Talil after having been hit by an Iraqi Surface-to-Air Missile (SAM), which destroyed his right engine. At least three A-10s suffered major battle damage during the campaign, but proved their survivability by returning to base. Another Battle Creek A-10, flown by Major Jim Ewald, was shot down, but Ewald ejected and was recovered by US forces. (USAF by SSgt Shane A. Cuomo)

SRA Christopher York of the 363rd Expeditionary Equipment Maintenance Squadron (EEMS) puts fins on AGM-88 High-Speed Anti-Radiation Missiles (HARMs) prior to loading aboard F-16CJ Wild Weasel aircraft on 25 March 2003. US aircraft fired 408 HARMs during Operation IRAQI FREEDOM and were largely responsible for the almost complete shutdown of Iraqi missile guidance systems. (USAF by SSgt Matthew Hansen)

An A-10 crew chief prepares to pull the chocks when given the signal for the big 'Warthog' to taxi. A AGM-65 Maverick is mounted on the wing pylon. Thunderbolt IIs were extremely effective in the CAS mission and in hunting and killing Iraqi armor. They operated at low altitude and often came back with the evidence of Iraqi hits. (USAF)

Crew chiefs from the 392nd AEW perform preflight checks on their A-10A prior to a 31 March 2003 mission from Talil AB, Iraq. Although the 'Warthog' is capable of dropping the Paveway series of LGBs using its Pave Penny targeting pod, its bomb of choice during Operation IRAQI FREEDOM was the Mark 80 series of 'dumb bombs.' These munitions rely on the pilot's skill to hit the target. (USAF by SSgt Shane A. Cuomo)

SSgt Rob Gray of the 386th AEW's transient alert team marshals an A-10A to its parking spot. The 'Warthog' is from the 172nd FS, 110th FW, Michigan Air National Guard (ANG) at Battle Creek ANG Base. It was assigned to the 332nd AEG for Operation IRAQI FREEDOM. (USAF by SSgt Karen J. Tomasik)

An A-10A assigned to the 332nd AEW taxis in after a 29 March Operation IRAQI FREEDOM mission. It did not expend the ordnance mounted under its wings during this sortie. The Thunderbolt IIs standard CAS load included a pair of AGM-65 Maverick Air-to-Surface Missiles (ASMs), AIM-9 Sidewinder Air-to-Air Missiles (AAMs), Mk 82 or 83 bombs, and the 30MM GAU-8/A Avenger cannon. Two F/A-18 Hornet fighters and a C-130 Hercules transport are parked further aft. (USAF by SRA JoAnn S. Makinano)

A flight of four F-16Cs from the 52nd FW at Spangdahlem AB, Germany fly observation formation off the port wing of a McDonnell Douglas KC-10A Extender. The KC-10A was from the 305th/514th Air Mobility Wing (AMW) at McGuire AFB, New Jersey. The Wing was deployed to Bourgas, Bulgaria to support tanker operations prior to and during Operation IRAQI FREEDOM. The F-16s are configured for the Suppression of Enemy Air Defenses (SEAD or 'Wild Weasel') role, with AIM-7 and AIM-120 AAMs and AGM-88 HARM. They also carry an AN/ALQ-131 jamming pod. (USAF by MSgt Dave Ahlschwede)

(Right) An F-16C pilot signals the boom operator as he takes on fuel. The F-16 has become the world's most prolific fighter today, with well over 2000 Fighting Falcons (a.k.a. 'Vipers') in USAF service and 2000 more serving in 23 other countries. (USAF)

LtCol Bob Broderick, 555th Fighter Squadron Commander and SRA Margarethe Via, a crew chief with the 555th, preflight an LGB on an F-16 prior to a mission. The 'Triple Nickel' was deployed from Aviano AB, Italy to Incirlik AB, Turkey, in support of Operation NORTHERN WATCH, which monitored and enforced the Northern No Fly Zone of Iraq prior to IRAQI FREEDOM. Both NORTHERN WATCH and SOUTHERN WATCH (over the Southern No Fly Zone) became a war in everything but name as Operation IRAQI FREEDOM approached and Iraqi Anti-Aircraft (AA) sites became more active. (USAF by SRA Ashley Sorrels)

SSgt Jerry Taylor, a crew chief with the 363rd Expeditionary Aircraft Maintenance Squadron (EAMS), checks an F-16CJ prior to an Operation IRAQI FREEDOM mission. He was deployed from 77th FS at Shaw AFB, South Carolina. (USAF by SSgt Matthew Hannen)

Maintainers with the 410th AEW test avionics on an F-16C prior to a 23 March 2003 Operation IRAQI FREEDOM mission. F-16s mission-capable rates during IRAQI FREEDOM varied from 73.9 percent for the F-16C+ to 84 percent for the F-16CG and 80.4 percent for the F-16CJ. (USAF by SSgt Samuel A. Park)

Maj Dan Gernert, an F-16CJ pilot deployed from Shaw AFB, adjusts his oxygen mask prior to an Operation IRAQI FREEDOM mission on 27 March 2003. F-16s operated from Al Jaber AB, Kuwait and Prince Sultan AB, Saudi Arabia during the conflict with Iraq. (USAF by SSgt Matthew Hannen)

Capt Jeremy Quatacker checks his preflight forms before an Operation IRAQI FREEDOM mission. Quatacker flew the F-16CG with the 524th EFS, out of Prince Sultan AB, Saudi Arabia. Seven different USAF fighter squadrons provided aircraft and pilots to the Air Expeditionary units fighting the air war. (USAF by MSgt Stefan Alford)

Armament specialists lift a Ford AIM-9 Sidewinder Air-to-Air Missile (AAM) for loading on an F-16. The Sidewinder was the first AAM in the US inventory and has remained a front-line munition through several upgrades, which have improved range and the acquisition envelope. It remains a heat-seeker, but the latest versions feature all-aspect acquisition capabilities. (USAF)

F-16s assumed the 'Wild Weasel' SAM-hunting/killing mission – officially known as Suppression of Enemy Air Defenses (SEAD) – after the F-4G Phantom II's retirement. Typical armament includes AIM-9 and AIM-120 AAMs, AGM-88 HARMs, and the AN/ALQ-184 Electronic Attack Pod. The High-Speed Anti-Radiation Missile (HARM) is a supersonic air-to-surface tactical missile designed to seek and destroy enemy radar-equipped air defense systems. The AGM-88 has been in production since 1983, and was previously carried by the McDonnell Douglas F-4G Phantom II.

An F-16 crew chief checks armament loads prior to a mission. The Viper is loaded with AIM-120 AAMs on the outboard stations and AGM-88 HARMs on the numbers 3 and 7 wing stations. The HARM is a follow-on to the Vietnam-era AGM-45 Shrike and is both longer and larger in diameter than the Shrike. US aircraft fired 408 HARMs during Operation IRAQI FREEDOM. (USAF)

Capt Matt Ayres, an F-16C pilot of the 363rd AEW, accepts several American flags prior to takeoff on a 27 March Operation IRAQI FREEDOM mission. The flags were displayed in the cockpit during the flight. Ayres deployed with the 77th FS, 363rd FW from Shaw AFB, South Carolina. Unit and name patches were removed from flight suits before combat missions for security reasons if the pilot was shot down and captured. (USAF by SSgt Matthew Hannen)

Capt Ayres' F-16C displays symbols for five HARM launches against Iraqi SAM sites later in the war. AGM-88 HARM missiles weigh 800 pounds (363 KG), including a 143 pound (65 KG) warhead. They are 13 feet 8 inches (4.2 M) long, ten inches (25.4 CM) in diameter, and have a wingspan of 3 feet 8 inches (1.1 M). The HARM has a range of up to 30 miles (48 KM) and a unit cost of $316,856. (USAF by SSgt Matthew Hannen)

F-16CJs from the 20th FW at Shaw AFB were deployed to the 363rd AEW. They are sitting out a sandstorm at Al Jaber AB, Kuwait on 26 March. These conditions slowed the Coalition march to Baghdad, but not for long. Middle Eastern conditions made orifice covers and sand filters essential for aircraft and support equipment. (USAF by SSgt Matthew Hannen)

A Boeing (McDonnell Douglas) F-15E Strike Eagle moves into position to receive fuel from a KC-135 during Operation SOUTHERN WATCH. This was a US and British program of air patrols over Southern Iraq's No-Fly Zone, which began after the 1991 Persian Gulf War. (NORTHERN WATCH monitored the Northern No-Fly Zone.) The F-15E is armed with 500 pound (227 KG) GBU-12 LGBs. The Low-Altitude Navigation and Targeting Infrared for Night (LANTIRN) pods mounted under the F-15E's engine intakes direct these weapons to the target. (USAF by SSgt Derrick C. Goode)

A 363rd AEW crew chief prepares an F-15E for an Operation IRAQI FREEDOM mission. F-15Es were stationed at Prince Sultan AB, Saudi Arabia. A pair of 25,000 pound thrust Pratt & Whitney F100-PW-220 engines power the Strike Eagle. The tailhook retracted between the engines engaged arresting cables strung across the runway in the event of a brake failure. (USAF by SSgt Derrick C. Goode)

Capts Tally Parham and Mary Melfi and 1/Lt Julie Ayres walk down the flightline at a forward-deployed air base in the Middle East on 3 May 2003. The three officers are assigned to the 379th AEW and flew combat missions during Operation IRAQI FREEDOM. Ayres and Melfi are F-15E Strike Eagle Weapons System Officers (WSOs) deployed from the 336th Expeditionary Fighter Squadron (EFS) at Seymour Johnson AFB, North Carolina. Parham is an F-16 Fighting Falcon pilot from the 157th EFS, South Carolina ANG at McEntire ANGB. (USAF by SSgt Derrick C. Goode)

A weapons load crew from the 22nd Expeditionary Fighter Squadron (EFS) mounts a GBU-31 on an F-16C prior to a 24 March 2003 mission. This Fighting Falcon was assigned to the 332nd AEG at Al Jaber AB, Kuwait. All USAF attack aircraft except the A-10 can carry the GBU-31. It has a nominal range of 22 miles (35 KM) and a Circular Error Probability (CEP) of 13 feet (4 M). (USAF by SSgt Derrick C. Goode)

SRA Mackenzie Wright loads a GBU-12 LGB on an F-15E prior to a night mission on 30 March 2003. He is a weapons specialist with the 334th EFS from Seymour Johnson AFB. Wright is wearing his Kevlar helmet without the usual camouflage cover, which matches his desert camouflage uniform. F-15Es carry ordnance on hardpoints on the wing undersurfaces, the lower surfaces of the conformal fuel tanks, and on the centerline. (USAF by SSgt Derrick C. Goode)

'Paps,' an F-16CJ pilot with the 169th FW of the South Carolina ANG, was deployed with the 157th EFS of the 379th AEW. (USAF withheld his real name for security reasons during Operation IRAQI FREEDOM, allowing only his call sign to be used.) He is checking one of his wingtip-mounted AIM-120 AMRAAMs prior to a mission from Al Udeid AB, Qatar. The USAF constructed this base – possibly the best in the Persian Gulf region – in 1996. This facility aids in hosting pre-positioned equipment for an Army brigade supporting an air expeditionary force consisting of 30 fighters and four tankers. (USAF by SMSgt Edward E. Snyder)

A Lockheed Martin U-2S 'Dragon Lady' flown by LtCol Walter Flint takes off for a mission on 11 April 2003. Flint was deployed from the 99th Reconnaissance Squadron (RS) at Beale AFB, California to the 363rd Expeditionary Reconnaissance Squadron (ERS) in the Persian Gulf region. The U-2R first flew in 1981 and is 40 percent larger than the original U-2. That initial variant was designed by Lockheed's Clarence L. 'Kelly' Johnson and first flew in August of 1955. U-2Rs were reengined and redesignated U-2Ss in the 1990s. (USAF by SSgt Matthew Hannen)

A Lockheed Martin F-117 Nighthawk pulls onto the tarmac at Holloman AFB, New Mexico on 16 April 2003. It has just returned with four other F-117s from Southwest Asia after supporting Operation IRAQI FREEDOM. This aircraft displays 16 combat mission marks showing the number of combat missions it flew during the deployment. The F-117 was the first aircraft designed to employ low observable (stealth) technology. It was a star of the first Gulf War, where it flew missions over Baghdad into an intense air defense environment without loss of a single aircraft. The Nighthawk's gross weight is 52,500 pounds (23,814 KG). (USAF by A1C Vanessa LaBoy)

An F-117 from the 8th EFS from Holloman AFB flies over the Persian Gulf on 14 April 2003. The 8th EFS returned to Holloman after having been deployed to Al Udeid AB, Qatar for Operation IRAQI FREEDOM. The USAF has 36 F-117s (out of 54 manufactured) in the active combat aircraft inventory. (USAF by SSgt Derrick C. Goode)

(Above) Maj John Long waits to be pressurized during a preflight pressure suit check prior to a U-2 mission on 13 April 2003. He is a pilot deployed from the 99th RS at Beale AFB to the 363rd ERS. The U-2S is a high-altitude Multi-Intelligence (MULTI-INT) reconnaissance aircraft. It can fly above 70,000 feet (21,336 M) and provides near-real-time imagery and signals intelligence to war fighters and national authorities in support of Operation IRAQI FREEDOM at a forward-deployed location in Southwest Asia. (USAF by SSgt Matthew Hannen)

(Below) Air Force members deployed from the 9th Aircraft Maintenance Squadron (AMS), Beale AFB to the 363rd Expeditionary Aircraft Maintenance Squadron (EAMS), refuel a U-2S after a mission on 13 April 2003. The US military often used the euphemism 'forward-deployed location.' This protects host countries and preserves security during operations without revealing the actual location. This U-2's 'forward-deployed location' was Al Dhafra AB, the United Arab Emirates (UAE). (USAF by SSgt Matthew Hannen)

Operation IRAQI FREEDOM was managed from Doha, Qatar, the headquarters of US Central Command (CENTCOM) and the Coalition of nations committed to ending Saddam Hussein's regime. Coalition troops track an ongoing mission in Southwest Asia at this Combined Air Operation Center (CAOC) at a forward-deployed location on 12 March 2003. (USAF by SSgt Derrick C. Goode)

The CAOC is the nerve center for all air component missions in support of Operation IRAQI FREEDOM. With crews operating around the clock, the CAOC plans, monitors and directs joint search and rescue, theatre missile defense, time sensitive targeting, battlefield coordination, special operations support, sortie execution and other mission critical operations. (USAF by SSgt Derrick C. Goode)

A Central Intelligence Agency (CIA)-controlled General Atomics MQ-1 Predator Unmanned Aerial Vehicle (UAV) fired an AGM-114 Hellfire missile on 4 November 2002. This strike killed six al-Qaeda members traveling in a vehicle in Yemen. Among those reported killed was Ali Qaed Senyan al-Harethi, a key suspect in the 12 October 2000 attack on the US destroyer COLE (DDG-67) in Aden Harbor, Yemen. Al-Harithi – the senior al-Qaeda leader in Yemen – was riding in a car along with five other alleged terrorists. The Hellfire hit the vehicle approximately 106 miles (171 KM) east of Yemen's capital Sana'a. The MQ-1B was flown by a pilot on the ground in French-garrisoned Djibouti and overseen by commanders in Saudi Arabia. Other Predators were employed on reconaissance over Iraq during Operation IRAQI FREEDOM. The Predator is powered by a 101 HP Rotax 912 four-cylinder pusher engine and has a gross takeoff weight of 2100 pounds (953 KG). (USAF by SSgt Jeremy T. Lock)

A 15th ERS pilot and sensor operator are completing their final preflight checks on a MQ-1 Predator at Al Dhafra AB. The UAV taxied to the active runway for a mission over Iraq following this inspection. The Predator Medium Altitude Endurance (MAE) UAV was developed as an Advanced Concept Technology Demonstration (ACTD) from January of 1994 to June of 1996. It went operational with a deployment to support the Bosnian operations in 1996. This Predator is armed with an AGM-114 Hellfire missile. Predators can operate for up to 24 hours at altitudes of up to 26,000 feet (7925 M), cruising at speeds between 70 knots (81 MPH/130 KMH) and 90 knots (104 MPH/167 KMH). They have an auto-return to base in case of data link loss. (USAF by Capt John Sheets)

SSgt Shawn Abrams, a crew chief with the 621st Air Mobility Group's Tanker Airlift Control Element, marshals a C-130 from it's parking spot at Talil AB in Southern Iraq on 1 April 2003. The remarkable Lockheed Martin C-130 Hercules maintained a 92 percent mission readiness rate throughout Operation IRAQI FREEDOM. (USAF by SSgt Shane A. Cuomo)

(Left) An airborne trooper of the 173rd Airborne Brigade boards a Boeing C-17A Globemaster III prior to parachuting into a Kurdish-controlled area of northern Iraq. The first combat drop of paratroops from a C-17 involved 1000 troopers from this Brigade. They were air-dropped after Turkey denied US forces permission for overland crossing into Northern Iraq. (USAF by A1C Isaac G. L. Freeman)

C-17A Globemaster IIIs are lined up at Ramstein AB, Germany waiting to transport US Army personnel forward during Operation IRAQI FREEDOM on 26 March 2003. The C-17 is now the heart of USAF airlift capability. It is able to land a cargo of 160,000 pounds (72,576 KG) on an unimproved airstrip as short as 3000 feet (914 M). (USAF by TSgt Stephen Faulisi)

A C-130 Hercules drops US Army and Kyrgyz National Guard troops over a drop zone at Frunze Field outside Bishkek, the capital of Kyrgyzstan. The 777th Expeditionary Airlift Squadron (EAS) and members of the 376th Air Expeditionary Wing (AEW) provided support to this joint exercise. This and other operations enhanced cooperation among Coalition forces during Operation IRAQI FREEDOM. (USAF by SRA Ashley Center)

(Right) A C-130 from the 64th Air Expeditionary Group (AEG) is loaded with cargo on 17 March 2003 at an undisclosed location. The USAF deployed 124 C-130s for intratheater airlift during Operation IRAQI FREEDOM. (USAF by SSgt Shane A. Cuomo)

A C-17A takes off from Mihail Kogalniceanu AB, Romania bound for CENTCOM's Area of Responsibility (AOR). The Globemaster III is assigned to the 458th AEG, which is maintaining an airbridge at the Romanian base for transporting supplies and personnel to the Persian Gulf region. (USAF by SRA Lakisha Croley)

A1C Brandon Midthun mans his .50 caliber (12.7MM) tail gun aboard a Sikorsky MH-53M PAVE LOW IV helicopter during a combat mission over Iraq. He is an aerial gunner assigned to the 21st Special Operations Squadron (SOS), which is based at Royal Air Force (RAF) Mildenhall, England. (USAF by SSgt Jerry Morrison)

A Sikorsky HH-60G PAVE HAWK awaits its next mission. This aircraft's primary wartime missions are Combat Search and Rescue (CSAR), infiltration and exfiltration, and resupply of Special Operations Forces (SOFs). The PAVE HAWK operates day or night and in marginal weather conditions. (USAF)

(Above) A Pararescue Jumper (PJ) stands near an MC-130P COMBAT SHADOW aircraft at a forward-deployed location. PJs airdrop behind enemy lines to aid shot down flight crews and get them aboard CSAR helicopters. (USAF by SSgt Shane A. Cuomo)

(Below) An HH-60G PAVE HAWK refuels from a 301st RQS MC-130P COMBAT SHADOW over southern Iraq on 6 April 2003. This team was credited with several saves of downed airmen and surrounded troops in combat during the war. (USAF by SSgt Shane A. Cuomo)

An MH-53J PAVE LOW III flies low over southern Iraq on an Operation IRAQI FREEDOM mission. PAVE LOW IIIs perform low-level, long-range, undetected penetration into denied areas, day or night, in adverse weather, for infiltration, exfiltration and resupply of SOFs. It is the USAF's largest and most powerful helicopter. (USAF)

An EC-130H COMPASS CALL aircraft from the 41st Expeditionary Electronic Combat Squadron (EECS) refuels while flying a mission over Iraq. This Squadron operated from Ali Al Salem AB, Kuwait during Operation IRAQI FREEDOM. COMPASS CALL aircraft employ their RIVET FIRE jamming suite to disrupt enemy Command, Control, and Communications (C^3) systems. (USAF by MSgt Luis Drummond)

The pilot of a 301st RQS HH-60G PAVE HAWK checks the starboard 7.62MM Minigun with the flight engineer. The two window-mounted guns are augmented by two door-mounted .50 caliber (12.7MM) machine guns. The rescue hoist above the cabin door has a 200-foot (61 M) cable and a 600-pound (272 KG) lift capability. (USAF by SSgt Shane A. Cuomo)

Two 301st RQS pararescuemen return with a downed pilot from a successful rescue mission on 8 April 2003. These men were taken aboard an MH-60G PAVE HAWK and flown to a forward-deployed location in southern Iraq. The HH-60G is capable of independent rescue operations in combat areas up to and including medium-threat environments. Recoveries are made by landing or by alternate means, such as rope ladder or hoist. Low-level tactical flight profiles are used to avoid threats. Night Vision Goggle (NVG) and Forward Looking Infrared (FLIR) assist low-level night operations and specially trained crews to perform night water operation missions. The basic crew normally consists of five: pilot, co-pilot, flight engineer, and two PJs. The aircraft can also carry eight to ten troops. (USAF by SSgt Shane A. Cuomo)

A USAF KC-135R refuels a Boeing F/A-18C Hornet over the CENTCOM AOR. This Hornet is assigned to Marine Fighter Attack Squadron One One Five (VMFA-115), Carrier Air Wing Three (CVW-3), embarked on the aircraft carrier USS HARRY S. TRUMAN (CVN-75). The ranges involved in Operation IRAQI FREEDOM strikes by carrier-based fighters required aerial refueling support from USAF tankers configured for the Navy-style probe and drogue refueling method. (USAF aircraft are configured for the receptacle and boom system.) (USN)

A McDonnell Douglas KC-10A Extender refuels an F-15E Strike Eagle while four more F-15Es maintain formation. The KC-10A's primary mission is aerial refueling, but it can combine the tasks of tanker and cargo aircraft by refueling fighters while carrying the fighters' support people and equipment during overseas deployments. The USAF deployed 33 KC-10As for IRAQI FREEDOM. (USAF)

A KC-10A deployed from McGuire AFB, New Jersey resumes its flight pattern after receiving fuel from a KC-135 Stratotanker over Afghanistan on 17 March 2003. The KC-135 crew from the 931st ARG at McConnell AFB, Kansas is currently assigned to the 405th AEW, forward-deployed location in Southwest Asia. Operation ENDURING FREEDOM in Afghanistan occurred simultaneously with Operation IRAQI FREEDOM. (USAF by SSgt Cherie A. Thurpoundy)

A 398th AEG RC-135V RIVET JOINT reconnaissance aircraft takes off from a forward-deployed location during the Iraq war. RIVET JOINT is the USAF's primary airborne reconnaissance platform providing data to theater commanders and national command authorities. This data is essential for effective combat operations. RC-135V crews also directly support combat operations through information warfare support. Additionally, they perform direction finding and range estimations in support of search and rescue operations. (USAF by TSgt Robert J. Horstman)

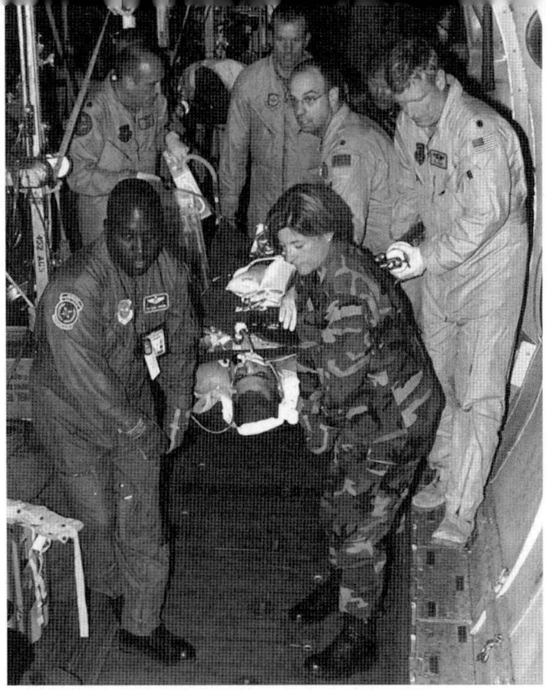

(Above) Wounded US personnel are loaded aboard an air evacuation aircraft in Iraq. Most wounded were evacuated from the CENTCOM AOR to Ramstein AB, Germany for long-term care after being stabilized in theater. (USAF)

(Above Right) A Boeing E-3B Sentry Airborne Warning And Control System (AWACS) aircraft flies over the CENTCOM AOR during the campaign. This aircraft provides all-weather surveillance, command, control and communications needed by commanders of US and North Atlantic Treaty Organization (NATO) air defense forces. The E-3 is a modified Boeing 707-320 commercial airframe with a rotating radar dome. This dome is 30 feet (9.1 M) in diameter, six feet (1.8 M) thick, and is held 11 feet (3.4 M) above the fuselage by two struts. It contains a radar subsystem that permits surveillance from the Earth's surface up into the stratosphere, over land or water. The radar has a range of more than 200 miles (322 KM) for low-flying targets and farther for aerospace vehicles flying at medium to high altitudes. The radar combined with an identification friend or foe subsystem can look down to detect, identify and track enemy and friendly low-flying aircraft by eliminating ground clutter returns that confuse other radar systems. (USAF)

(Right) SRA Madrid, an MC-130P COMBAT SHADOW crewman, conducts a Pressure, Regulator, Inspection, Connection, Emergency (PRICE) check. This procedure occurred prior to engine startup at a forward-deployed location during Operation IRAQI FREEDOM. This airman was assigned to the 67th Special Operations Squadron (SOS). The MC-130P (formerly the HC-130P/N) COMBAT SHADOW flies clandestine or low visibility, low-level missions into politically sensitive or hostile territory to provide air refueling for special operations helicopters. Special Operations were a large component of Operation IRAQI FREEDOM. (USAF by SSgt Jerry Morrison)

Aircrew from the 398th AEG walk towards a RC-135V RIVET JOINT at a forward-deployed operating base located in the Mediterranean region. A US Navy Lockheed EP-3E Orion Electronic Intelligence (ELINT) aircraft is parked in the background. The RC-135V has a minimum crew of 24, which includes pilot and copilot, two navigators, three electronic warfare officers and a maintenance technician, all assigned to Air Combat Command (ACC). Also aboard are 15 enlisted operators and one maintenance technician, who are assigned to the Air Intelligence Agency (AIA). (USAF by TSgt Robert J. Horstman)

(Above) A motivational message that needs no elaboration, this was painted on the superstructure of an unknown US Navy warship. This vessel was one of many US Navy ships deployed to the CENTCOM AOR for Operation IRAQI FREEDOM. (USN)

(Above Left) The SPRUANCE Class destroyer USS DEYO (DD-989) conducts underway operations on 29 March 2003. DEYO was one of many US Navy surface combatants to fire Tomahawk Land Attack Missiles (TLAMS) in support of Operation IRAQI FREEDOM. The addition of the Mk 41 Vertical Launch System (VLS) or Tomahawk Armored Box Launchers (ABLs) to many SPRUANCE Class destroyers has greatly expanded the destroyer's role in strike warfare. (USN by CJO Alan J. Baribeau)

(Left) A tug guides the amphibious assault ship USS IWO JIMA (LHD-7) from the pier at Naval Station (NS) Norfolk, Virginia on 4 March 2003. She is departing on a deployment to the CENTCOM AOR. The banner on her port stern quotes President George W. Bush: *"We will not tire, we will not falter, we will not fail."* (USN by PH2 Benjamin Hammond)

(Below) The NIMITZ Class nuclear-powered aircraft carrier USS HARRY S. TRUMAN (CVN-75) conducts flight operations in the Mediterranean Sea on 20 March 2003. An F/A-18 Hornet has launched from one of TRUMAN's two waist catapults. Other aircraft from Carrier Air Wing Three (CVW-3) are spotted on the flight deck. (USN by PH2 Richard A. Virginia)

(Above) HARRY S. TRUMAN steams in the Eastern Mediterranean Sea on 29 March 2003. She embarked CVW-3 during her deployment in support of Operation IRAQI FREEDOM. This Wing included the following Squadrons and aircraft: VF-32 (F-14); VMFA-115, VFA-37, and VFA-105 (all F/A-18); VAQ-130 (EA-6B), VAW-126 (E-2C), HS-7 (SH-60F/HH-60H), VS-22 (S-3B), and VRC-40/Det. 3 (C-2A). TRUMAN commissioned at NS Norfolk on 25 July 1998. (USN by PH1 Michael W. Pendergrass)

(Right) TRUMAN turns sharply to port to put the wind down the angle deck in preparation for the start of flight operations on 31 March 2003. The carrier's two nuclear reactors give her virtually unlimited range and endurance and a top speed in excess of 30 knots (35 MPH/56 KMH). Eight steam turbine generators each produce 8000 kilowatts of electrical power. The ship has enough electrical generating power to supply electricity to a city of 100,000. (USN by PH1 Michael W. Pendergrass)

USS THEODORE ROOSEVELT (CVN-71) receives cargo while pierside at the NATO Marathi Pier Facility at Souda Bay, Crete on 4 March 2003. The carrier – nicknamed 'Big Stick' – and her CVW-8 were taking on supplies in preparation for the beginning of Operation IRAQI FREEDOM. CVW-8 consisted of VF-213 (F-14D), VFA-201 (F/A-18A), VFA-15 (F/A-18C), VFA-87 (F/A-18C), VAQ-141 (EA-6B), VAW-124 (E-2C), HS-3 (SH-60F/HH-60H), VS-24 (S-3B), VRC-40/Det. 1 (C-2A). (USN by PH1 Michael W. Pendergrass)

US CENTCOM – Navies

Air Order of Battle

Unit	Squadron	Aircraft
Shore-Based Units		
	HS817 Sq [RAN]	1 H-3
	HM-15 Blackhawks	10 MH-53s
	HM-5 Blackhawks	MH-53s
	VP-1 Screaming Eagles	P-3s
	Det. VQ-1 World Watchers	EP-3E ARIES IIs
	Det. Two HC-2 Fleet Angels	UH-3Hs
		VH-3As
	Det. One HC-4 Black Stallions	MH-53Es
	Det A, VMGR-452 Yankees	KC-130Ts
	VMFA-251 Thunderbolts	12 F/A-18Cs
	VMFA(AW)-533 Hawks	12 F/A-18Ds
CVN-71 USS THEODORE ROOSEVELT		
Carrier Air Wing 8		
	VF-213 Blacklions	10 F-14Ds
	VFA-15 Valions	12 F/A-18Cs
	VFA-87 War Party	12 F/A-18Cs
	VFA-201 Hunters	12 F/A-18As
	VMFA-312 Hunters	12 F/A-18Cs
	VAW-124 Bear Aces	4 E-2Cs
	VAQ-141 Shadowhawks	4 EA-6Bs
	VS-24 Scouts	8 S-3Bs
	VRC-40 Rawhides Det. 1	2 C-2As
CVN-68 USS NIMITZ		
Carrier Air Wing 11		
	VFA-14 Tophatters	12 F/A-18s
	VFA-41 Black Aces	12 F/A-18s
	VFA-94 Mighty Shrikes	12 F/A-18s
	VFA-97 Warhawks	12 F/A-18s
	VAW-117 Wallbangers	4 E-2Cs
	VAQ-135 Black Ravens	4 EA-6Bs
	VS-29 Dragonfires	8 S-3Bs
	VRC-30 Providers Detatchment	2 C-2As
	HS-6 Indians	4 SH-60Fs
		2 HH-60Hs
CVN-72 USS ABRAHAM LINCOLN		
Carrier Air Wing 14		
	VF-31 Tomcatters	F-14Ds
	VFA-25 Fist of the Fleet	F/A-18Es
	VFA-113 Stingers	F/A-18Cs
	VFA-115 Eagles	F/A-18Es
	VAW-113 Black Eagles	E-2Cs
	VAQ-139 Cougars	EA-6Bs
	VS-35 Blue Wolves	S-3Bs
	HS-4 Black Knight	SH-60s
	VRC-30 Providers Det. 1	C-2As
CVN-75 USS HARRY S. TRUMAN		
Carrier Air Wing 3		
	VF-32 Swordsmen	F-14s
	VMFA-115 Silver Eagles	F/A-18s
	VFA-37 Bulls	F/A-18s
	VFA-105 Gunslingers	F/A-18s
	VAQ-130 Zappers	EA-6Bs
	VAW-126 Seahawks	E-2Cs
	HS-7 Big Dippers	SH-60Fs/HH-60Hs
	VS-22 Vidars	S-3Bs
	VRC-40 Rawhides Det. 3	C-2As

Unit	Squadron	Aircraft
CV-63 USS KITTY HAWK		
Carrier Air Wing 5		
	VF-154 Black Knights	F-14As
	VFA-27 Royal Maces	F/A-18Cs
	VFA-192 Golden Dragons	F/A-18Cs
	VFA-195 Dambusters	F/A-18Cs
	VAQ-136 Gauntlets	EA-6Bs
	VAW-115 Liberty Bells	E-2Cs
	VS-21 Fighting Redtails	S-3Bs
	HS-14 Chargers	SH-60s/HH-60s
	VRC-30 Providers Det. 5	C-2As
CV-64 USS CONSTELLATION		
Carrier Air Wing 2		
	VF-2 Bounty Hunters	F-14s
	VFA-137 Kestrels	F/A-18s
	VFA-151 Vigilantes	F/A-18s
	VMFA-323 Death Rattlers	F/A-18s
	VAQ-131 Lancers	EA-6Bs
	VAW-116 Sun Kings	E-2Cs
	VS-38 Red Griffins	S-3Bs
	HS-2 Golden Falcons	SH-60s
	VRC-30 Providers Det. 2	C-2As
LHA-4 USS NASSAU		
	HMM-263 Thunder Chickens	12 CH-46s
		4 CH-53Es
		3 UH-1Ns
		4 AH-1Ws
		6 AV-8Bs
LHA-1 USS TARAWA		
	HMM-161 Greyhawks	12 CH-46s
		4 CH-53Es
		3 UH-1Ns
		4 AH-1Ws
		6 AV-8Bs
Amphibious Task Force - East		
	Marine Aircraft Group 29	
	HMH-464	CH-53Es
	HMM-162	CH-46E
	HMM-365	CH-46Es
	HMLA-269	UH-1Ns
		AH-1Ws
	VMA-223	AV-8B+s
	VMA-542	AV-8B+s
Amphibious Task Force - West		
	3rd Marine Aircraft Wing	
	Marine Aircraft Group 13	
	HMM-268	CH-46Es
	VMA-211	AV-8B+s
	VMA-311	AV-8B+s
	Marine Aircraft Group 39	
	HMLA-169	AH-1Ws
	HMLA-267	UH-1Ns

RAN – Royal Australian Navy
HM – Helicopter Mine Countermeasures Squadron
VP – Patrol Squadron
Det. – Detachment
VQ – Fleet Air Reconnaissance Squadron
HC – Helicopter Combat Support Squadron
VMGR – Marine Refueler Transport Squadron
VMFA – Marine Fighter Attack Squadron
VMFA(AW) – Marine Fighter Attack Squadron (All-Weather)
VF – Fighter Squadron
VFA – Strike Fighter Squadron
VAW – Airborne Early Warning Squadron
VAQ – Electronic Attack Squadron
VS – Sea Control Squadron
VRC – Fleet Logistics Support Squadron
HS – Helicopter Antisubmarine Squadron
HMM – Marine Helicopter Squadron, Medium
HMLA – Marine Helicopter Attack Squadron, Light
VMA – Marine Attack Squadron

A crewmember inspects the launch bar before an F/A-18C Hornet is launched from USS NIMITZ (CVN-68) in the Arabian (Persian) Gulf on 25 April 2003. The Hornet is assigned to the 'Mighty Shrikes' of Strike Fighter Squadron Ninety Four (VFA-94). (USN)

The Deputy Commander of CVW-14 adjusts his parachute harness as he prepares to launch from ABRAHAM LINCOLN. In an emergency, he is ejected in his seat. The aviator's personal parachute automatically deploys moments after he is separated from the ejection seat following ejection from the aircraft.

Aviation Ordnancemen move a Raytheon AGM-154A Joint Standoff Weapon (JSOW) to a nearby aircraft aboard USS ABRAHAM LINCOLN (CVN-72). JSOW can be used in adverse weather and gives aircrews the ability to attack multiple targets in a single sortie. The JSOW family uses a common weapon body for all variants. The AGM-154A carries BLU-97 combined-effect bomblets for use against area targets. (USN by PH3 Tyler J. Clements)

ABRAHAM LINCOLN's catapult officer (right, in yellow shirt and vest) checks all launch parameters prior to giving the signal to launch an aircraft on 29 March 2003. CVW-14 was embarked on LINCOLN and included VF-31 (F-14D), VFA-115 (F/A-18E), VFA-113 (F/A-18C), VFA-25 (F/A-18C), VAQ-139 (EA-6B), VAW-113 (E-2C), HS-4 (SH-60F/HH-60H), VS-35 (S-3B), VRC-30/Det. 1 (C-2A). LINCOLN joined the fleet in 1990 when USS CORAL SEA (CV-43) was decommissioned. (USN by PH3 Tyler J. Clements)

VFA-105 Aviation Ordnancemen ('Ordies') transfer several 1000 pound (454 KG) Boeing GBU-35(V)-1/B Joint Direct Attack Munitions (JDAMs) to their aircraft. The Squadron was embarked on HARRY S. TRUMAN during operations against Iraq. Navy bomb cases have rough coatings to prevent bomb explosions during fires aboard the ship. (USN by PH1 Michael W. Pendergrass)

'Ordies' from VFA-37 'Bulls' transfer several Hughes AIM-120 Advanced Medium-Range Air-to-Air Missiles (AMRAAM) to aircraft on TRUMAN's flight deck. The AMRAAM weighs 340 pounds (154 KG) and uses an advanced solid-fuel rocket motor to achieve a speed of Mach 4 and a range exceeding 30 miles (48 KM). (USN by PH1 Michael W. Pendergrass)

Aviation Ordnancemen assigned to Fighter Squadron Thirty Two (VF-32) 'The Swordsmen' transfer 2000 pound (907 KG) JDAMs on TRUMAN's flight deck. These weapons were then loaded onto a Grumman F-14B Tomcat fighter aircraft on the carrier, which was steaming in the eastern Mediterranean during Operation ENDURING FREEDOM. (USN by PHA Justin S. Osborne)

Aviation Ordnancemen load a 2000 pound JDAM onto an F/A-18C Hornet spotted on TRUMAN's flight deck. These deck crews wear red helmets, shirts, and vests to easily distinguish themselves from other crewmen on the flight deck.

An Ordnanceman inspects a 20MM General Electric M61A1 Vulcan cannon after its removal from an F/A-18 Hornet aboard USS CONSTELLATION (CV-64) on 22 March 2003. The six-barrel rotary cannon with 520 rounds of 20MM ammunition is internally mounted in the Hornet's nose. The M61A1 Vulcan has a maximum firing rate of 6000 rounds per minute and a muzzle velocity of 3380 feet (1030 M) per second. This weapon is employed for both air-to-air and air-to-surface combat. (USN by PHA John P. Curtis)

A Naval Aviator makes his way to his aircraft prior to an IRAQI FREEDOM mission. He is wearing a torso harness, which will attach him to the aircraft's ejection seat. This aviator also wears an anti-g (gravity) suit on his lower torso and legs, a survival vest with a wide variety of items, and a flotation collar. (USN)

Hangar bays on most carriers were used as staging areas for a variety of ordnance during Operation IRAQI FREEDOM. Truckloads of 500 pound (227 KG) GBU-12 Laser-Guided Bombs (LGBs) – the most popular bomb during this campaign – are arranged in the Hangar bay of USS KITTY HAWK (CV-63). The weapons were loaded aboard F/A-18s and F-14s sent to attack Republican Guard positions in Iraq. KITTY HAWK embarked CVW-5, whose squadrons are: VF-154 (F-14A); VFA-27, VFA-192, and VFA-195 (all F/A-18C); VAQ-136 (EA-6B), VAW-115 (E-2C), HS-14 (SH-60F/HH-60H), VS-21 (S-3B), and VRC-30/Det. 5 (C-2A). (USN by JO1 Dwayne S. Smith)

JDAMs and LGBs are lined up on a carrier's flight deck before they are loaded for missions over Iraq. These 'smart' weapons comprised 80 percent of all bombs dropped on Iraq during Operation IRAQI FREEDOM. (USN)

An Aviation Boatswain's Mate directs an F/A-18E Super Hornet assigned to VFA-115 'Eagles' prior to its launch from ABRAHAM LINCOLN on 20 March 2003. The single-seat F/A-18E and two-seat F/A-18F are 4.2 feet (1.3 M) longer than earlier Hornets, have a 25 percent larger wing area, and carry 33 percent more internal fuel. This effectively increases the newer aircraft's mission range by 41 percent and endurance by 50 percent over F/A-18A through D variants. The Super Hornet also incorporates two additional weapon stations, which allow for increased payload flexibility by mixing and matching air-to-air and/or air-to-ground ordnance. Additionally, the F/A-18E/F can carry the complete complement of 'smart' weapons, including the newest joint weapons like JDAM and JSOW. (USN by PH3 Tyler Clements)

(Above) An F/A-18C Hornet assigned to VFA-105 'Gunslingers' launches from one of HARRY S. TRUMAN's four steam driven catapults. The Hornet has an intercept radius of over 400 miles (644 KM) without external fuel tanks. In the air-to-ground role, the F/A-18C can attack targets over 550 miles (885 KM) away and accurately deliver up to 17,000 pounds (7711 KG) of conventional bombs, precision munitions, air-to-surface missiles, cluster weapons, and rockets. The Hornet carries a mixed load of the most capable air-to-air missiles for the fighter role. This aircraft employs the highly effective 20MM Vulcan cannon on all missions.

A VFA-115 'Eagles' F/A-18C Hornet taxies to one of four catapults prior to launching from ABRAHAM LINCOLN. She and CVW-14 were conducting combat operations in support of Operation IRAQI FREEDOM. F/A-18C/Ds are reaching their specified design limits faster due to increased operational usage. The F/A-18C has become the carrier workhorse during the past decade, causing an accelerated wear out rate. (USN by PHA Tiffany A. Aiken)

An F/A-18C Hornet assigned to VFA-113 'Stingers' launches from ABRAHAM LINCOLN in the Persian Gulf on 20 March 2003. A Sikorsky HH-60 flies 'plane guard' off LINCOLN's bow, in case the Hornet has trouble during the launch. NIMITZ and ROOSEVELT-Class carriers can launch up to four aircraft per minute. The ship's four catapults and four arresting gear engines enable her to launch and recover aircraft both rapidly and simultaneously. (USN by PH3 Philip A. McDaniel)

Afterburners blazing, an F/A-18C is launched from a carrier's waist catapult. The F/A-18C/D is powered by two 18,000 pound thrust General Electric F404-GE-402 afterburning engines. This results in a combat thrust-to-weight ratio greater than 1-to-1. Depending on the mission and load, the F/A-18C's combat radius exceeds 500 nautical miles (576 miles/927 KM).

An F/A-18C launched from a carrier's waist catapult is caught at the moment of release from the shuttle. Powerful steam catapults (affectionately called 'Fat Cats') can accelerate 37-ton (34 MT) jets from zero to a safe flight speed of up to 180 MPH (290 KMH) in approximately 300 feet (91 M) and in less than three seconds. Each aircraft's weight determines the amount of thrust provided by the catapult.

An F/A-18C Hornet is chained to HARRY S. TRUMAN's flight deck awaiting its load of weapons. F/A-18Cs and two-seat F/A-18Ds are range-limited compared to the A-6s they replaced and all Hornets carried an extra 330 gallon (1249 L) external tank during Operation IRAQI FREEDOM missions. (USN by PHA Ryan O'Connor)

A Naval Aviator boards an F/A-18C prior to a night mission over Iraq. Flight operations at night are enhanced by the use of Night Vision Goggles (NVGs), which all pilots use while airborne. The ability to operate effectively in the dark is one of the most important advantages Coalition forces enjoyed over their Iraqi counterparts. There was virtually no time that the enemy could move without being spotted, either visually or using a variety of airborne sensors. (USN)

An F/A-18F Super Hornet assigned to VFA-41 'Black Aces' prepares to launch from NIMITZ on 22 March 2003. NIMITZ steamed from the Pacific Ocean to the Arabian Sea for Operation ENDURING FREEDOM. Pacific Fleet CVWs have two-letter tail codes beginning with N, while Atlantic Fleet CVWs have tail codes starting with A. (USN by AN Angel G. Hipoundrands)

An Airman checks the area surrounding an F/A-18E Super Hornet just prior to launching from ABRAHAM LINCOLN in the Persian Gulf on 1 April 2003. While on route to the Area of Operations, NIMITZ launched four Super Hornets from VFA-41 and VFA-14 on 30 March. They flew to LINCOLN since this carrier was short of fighter capacity. They were returned to CVW-11 aboard NIMITZ after major combat operations ended on 1 May. (USN by PH3 Tyler J. Clements)

A Naval Aviator aboard an F/A-18C Hornet waits to be launched from one of ABRAHAM LINCOLN's four steam powered catapults on 1 April 2003. The F/A-18 has a digital control-by-wire flight control system, which provides excellent handling qualities, and allows pilots to learn to fly the airplane with relative ease. F/A-18s feature a 'hands-off' launch system, which eases the pilot's workload under the high-g forces of catapult shots. (USN by AN Jeanine Garcia)

Pilots assigned to VFA-41 'Black Aces' egress from their F/A-18F Super Hornet and step onto ABRAHAM LINCOLN'S flight deck on 1 April 2003. NIMITZ lent four Super Hornets from her CVW-11 to LINCOLN's CVW-14. This move was unique in naval aviation, since both carriers were approximately 4000 miles (6437 KM) apart. CVW-11 tankers from NIMITZ refueled the aircraft for the first 1700 miles (2736 KM), then tankers from the USAF and LINCOLN refueled the Super Hornets the remaining 2300 miles (3701 KM). The F/A-18E/Fs first flew combat off LINCOLN on 9 April. This provided a mix of fighter/tanker capabilities to support coalition forces on the ground in Iraq. The Super Hornet's greater range and load-carrying capabilities led to its being used in the tanker role. All F/A-18s have integral crew access ladders, which retract into the port Leading Edge Extension (LEX). (USN by PH3 Philip A. McDaniel)

A VFA-25 'Fist of the Fleet' F/A-18C prepares to launch from ABRAHAM LINCOLN's flight deck on 5 April 2003. The 401 modex on the nose and tail indicates this aircraft is assigned to the Commanding Officer of a Strike Fighter Squadron. The raised Jet Blast Deflector aft of the Hornet shields personnel and equipment from the force of jet engine exhausts. (USN by PH3 Elizabeth A. Bartneck)

The names and flight numbers of the hijacked passenger flights are painted on the nose of this VFA-115 F/A-18E aboard LINCOLN. This was done to honor the memory of those who died in the 11 September 2001 terrorist attacks on the United States. The art is painted under the low-voltage formation light panels on the port nose. (USN by PH3 Michael S. Kelly)

VFA-115 'Eagles' Aviation Ordnancemen load weapons onto a VFA-41 'Black Aces' F/A-18F Super Hornet aboard LINCOLN in the Persian Gulf. The aircraft had just recovered aboard the carrier from its first combat mission on 1 April 2003. (USN by PH3 Philip A. McDaniel)

An F/A-18 Hornet assigned to VFA-94 'Mighty Shrikes' completes an arrested landing aboard NIMITZ during Operation IRAQI FREEDOM. Naval Aviators apply full power when their aircraft lands on a carrier. This allows them to safely get airborne if their tail hook fails to engage one of the carrier's arresting cables ('wires'). (USN by PH3 Yesenia Rosas)

(Above) An F/A-18C assigned to HARRY S. TRUMAN's CVW-3 refuels from a USAF KC-135R Stratotanker over the Middle East on 16 April 2003. The Hornet's refueling probe engages a basket fitted to the KC-135R's refueling boom. The KC-135R is assigned to the 196th Expeditionary Air Refueling Squadron (EARS), which is stationed at a forward-deployed airbase in the Mediterranean region. The USAF stationed tankers from Crete to Bulgaria and in several locations within the Persian Gulf region. (USAF by TSgt Robert J. Horstman)

(Left) Pilots assigned to VFA-192 'Golden Dragons' return to Naval Air Facility (NAF) Atsugi, Japan on 1 May 2003. They flew F/A-18Cs during CVW-5's deployment aboard KITTY HAWK in support of Operation IRAQI FREEDOM. KITTY HAWK is based at Yokosuka, Japan – the only non-US home port for a US Navy carrier. (USN by PH2 Joshua C. Millage)

(Above) A VF-213 'Black Lions' F-14 Tomcat (center) prepares to launch from THEODORE ROOSEVELT in the Mediterranean on 2 April 2003. An F/A-18 Hornet (right) assigned to VFA-201 is temporarily parked near a catapult. Both VF-213 and VFA-201 were assigned to CVW-8 aboard ROOSEVELT during Operation IRAQI FREEDOM (USN by PH2 James K. McNeil)

(Right) VFA-115 pilots walk toward waiting friends and family after returning to Naval Air Station (NAS) Lemoore, California on 1 May 2003. They were deployed with CVW-14 aboard ABRAHAM LINCOLN for nearly ten months in support of both Operations ENDURING FREEDOM in Afghanistan and IRAQI FREEDOM in Iraq. (USN by PH3 Greg Badger)

Three Grumman F-14A Tomcats fly in formation on their initial approach to KITTY HAWK on 3 April 2003. This Squadron was part of CVW-5 aboard KITTY HAWK for Operation IRAQI FREEDOM. (USN by PH3 Todd Frantom)

A flight deck director positions an F-14D Tomcat assigned to VF-31 'Tomcatters' for launch from ABRAHAM LINCOLN on 1 April 2003. This carrier cruised in the Persian Gulf during the Iraq conflict. Remaining F-14s are being outfitted with enhanced defensive countermeasure systems (Swedish-developed BOL chaff dispensers and the AN/ALR-67 Radar Warning Receiver), night vision capability, and Global Positioning System (GPS) receivers. (USN by PH3 Elizabeth A. Bartneck)

Bomb and missile mission tallies are painted below the canopy of this VF-2 'Bounty Hunters' F-14 aboard CONSTELLATION. These markings represented missions during Operation IRAQI FREEDOM. F-14s added precision strike to their primary fleet air defense role from late 1995. (USN by PH2 Felix Garza, Jr.)

A VF-32 'Swordsmen' F-14 is prepared for launch from HARRY S. TRUMAN in the Mediterranean on 28 March 2003. Tomcats are equipped with Low-Altitude Navigation and Targeting for Infra-Red at Night (LANTIRN) pods. These pods give the F-14 the capability to deliver Laser-Guided Bombs (LGBs) on precision strike missions. (USN by PH3 Danny Ewing, Jr.)

A Grumman EA-6B Prowler assigned to Electronic Attack Squadron One Three Six (VAQ-136) 'Gauntlets' prepares to recover aboard KITTY HAWK in the Persian Gulf on 28 March 2003. The EA-6B electronic warfare aircraft had played a key role in suppressing enemy air defenses during Operation DESERT STORM in 1991. The Prowler enhances the strike capabilities not only of carrier air wings but also of USAF and Allied forces. This aircraft is assigned all US Department of Defense radar jamming missions. (USN by PH3 Todd Frantom)

A VAQ-130 'Zappers' EA-6B launches from HARRY S. TRUMAN in the Mediterranean on 23 March 2003. The EA-6B's heart is the AN/ALQ-99 Tactical Jamming System. This aircraft can carry up to five jamming pods: one on the centerline and two under each wing. Each integrally powered pod houses two jamming transmitters that cover one of seven frequency bands. The EA-6B can carry any mix of pods, fuel tanks, and/or HARM anti-radiation missiles depending on mission requirements. (USN by PHA Ryan O'Connor)

A sailor aboard the fast combat support ship USS RAINIER (AOE-7) attaches a cargo hook to a Boeing Vertol CH-46D Sea Knight during a Vertical Replenishment (VERTREP) with ABRAHAM LINCOLN in the Persian Gulf. This aircraft is assigned to the 'Gunbearers' of Helicopter Combat Support Squadron Eleven Detachment Five (HC-11/Det. 5). Unusual orange and black flames are painted on the Sea Knight's nose and forward rotor housing. (USN by PHA Gabriel Piper)

A HC-6 'Chargers' CH-46D flies a VERTREP to the amphibious command and control ship USS MOUNT WHITNEY (LCC/JCC-20) in the Arabian Sea. The CH-46 Sea Knight has served the USN and Marine Corps faithfully since the early 1960s. This venerable aircraft's primary Navy mission areas include Combat Logistics Support and VERTREP, Search and Rescue, and Special Operations. (USN by CJO Robert Benson)

A patriotically marked CH-46D assigned to HC-11/Det. 5 performs a VERTREP between USS CAMDEN (AOE-2) and ABRAHAM LINCOLN. A net slung under the Sea Knight contains supplies bound for the carrier. (USN by PH2 Julie Matyascik)

A HC-11/Det. 5 CH-46D hovers above CAMDEN during a VERTREP and Connected Replenishment (CONREP) on 28 March 2003. A CONREP uses a high line between ships to transfer goods. The Navy Air Systems Command ordered all 291 CH-46s grounded on 18 August 2002, after a crack was found in a Sea Knight's rotor component at Marine Corps Air Station (MCAS) Cherry Point, North Carolina. A similar problem was found a few days later in a CH-46 deployed aboard the amphibious assault ship USS BELLEAU WOOD (LHA-3) in the Persian Gulf area. Inspections found only one Sea Knight with this type of flaw and the full fleet was returned to service. (USN by PH2 Julie Matyascik)

A HM-14 'Vanguards' MH-53E Sea Dragon lifts off at the beginning of a mine-sweeping mission in the Persian Gulf during Operation IRAQI FREEDOM. The newest military version of Sikorsky's H-53E/S-80 series, the MH-53E is the Western world's largest helicopter. It is used primarily for Airborne Mine Countermeasures (AMCM), with a secondary mission of shipboard delivery. AMCM missions include mine sweeping and ancillary spotting, mine neutralization, floating mine destruction, channel marking, and surface towing of small craft and ships. (USN)

(Left) An Aviation Boatswain's Mate signals the launch of a CH-53D Sea Stallion from the flight deck of the amphibious assault ship USS SAIPAN (LHA-2). This ship was one of several such vessels deployed to CENTCOM's Area of Responsibility (AOR) for the conflict with Iraq. (USN by PH3 Robert M Schalk)

A Sikorsky CH-53E Super Stallion assigned to the 'Condors' of Marine Heavy Helicopter Squadron Four Sixty Four (HMH-464) launches from the amphibious assault ship USS KEARSARGE (LHD-3) on 30 April 2003. This Squadron was part of Marine Air Group Twenty Nine (MAG-29), which was assigned to Amphibious Task Force – East. KEARSARGE was deployed in the Persian Gulf for Operation IRAQI FREEDOM. (USN by PH3 Jose E. Ponce)

(Below) Two Aviation Boatswain's Mates make final checks before launching an MH-53E Sea Dragon from SAIPAN in the Persian Gulf on 31 March 2003. The Sea Dragon is assigned to the 'Blackhawks' of Helicopter Mine Countermeasures Squadron Fifteen (HM-15). (USN by PH1 Courtney Torgrude)

Members of Commander Task Unit 55.4.3 (CTU-55.4.3) unload supplies during a sandstorm from a HM-14 MH-53E at Umm Qasr, Iraq on 27 March 2003. CTU-55.4.3 consists of US Naval Special Clearance Team-1, Explosive Ordnance Disposal Mobile Units 6 and 8, Fleet Diving Unit 3 from the United Kingdom, and a Clearance Dive Team from Australia. These units conducted deep/shallow water mine counter measure operations to clear shipping lanes. CTU-55.4.3 was instrumental in clearing the way for the British Royal Fleet Auxiliary landing ship RFA SIR GALAHAD (L-3005), which delivered the first wave of humanitarian aid in support of Operation IRAQI FREEDOM. (USN by PH2 Bob Houlihan)

A HM-14 MH-53E Sea Dragon pulls a Mk 105 magnetic sled during AMCM operations near the mouth of the Khawar Abd Allah river separating Iraq and Kuwait on 23 March 2003. The sled cruises on twin floats atop the water and has an electric motor to create magnetic fields, which are used to detonate the mines. This Squadron was repositioned aboard the AUSTIN Class amphibious warfare ship USS PONCE (LPD-15) in support of Operation IRAQI FREEDOM. (USN by PH1 Brien Aho)

A plane captain monitors engine start on a Grumman C-2A Greyhound assigned to Fleet Logistics Support Squadron Forty (VRC-40) 'Rawhides' on 26 March 2003. This Carrier Onboard Delivery (COD) aircraft deployed from NAS Norfolk, Virginia to USS HARRY S. TRUMAN (CVN-75). The C-2A is capable of carrying a mix of 10,000 pounds (4536 KG) of high-priority cargo and passengers. This COD can accommodate up to 26 passengers or up to 20 litter patients. (USN by PHA Carl E. Gibson)

Sailors assigned to Light Helicopter Anti-Submarine Squadron Forty Four (HSL-44) 'Swamp Foxes' service their Sikorsky SH-60B Seahawk on 23 March 2003. This helicopter is embarked aboard the guided missile cruiser USS CAPE ST. GEORGE (CG-71), which operated in the Mediterranean Sea during Operation IRAQI FREEDOM. (USN by PH1 Michael W. Pendergrass)

The catapult officer checks all aspects of safety before launching a Northrop Grumman E-2C Hawkeye from ABRAHAM LINCOLN (CVN-72). E-2Cs serve as the 'eyes and ears' for US carrier battle groups. They are equipped with long-range surveillance radar and have significant communication capability. One Carrier Airborne Early Warning Squadron (VAW) of four Hawkeyes is assigned to each CVW to serve as battle manager for the fleet. (USN by PH3 Tyler J. Clements)

(Left) AN Ray Marino signals the aircrew while starting up an E-2C aboard THEODORE ROOSEVELT (CVN-71) on 2 April 2003. The Hawkeye is assigned to VAW-124 'Bear Aces.' The E-2 serves in a similar role as that of the USAF E-3 AWACS. (USN by PH3 Matthew Bash)

(Below) A brown-shirted plane captain carries several heavy chains to secure aircraft to the flight deck. Working aircraft carrier flight decks is a dirty, dangerous, and exhausting job. The decks are often slippery and aircraft handlers must avoid prop and jet wash while ducking around and under aircraft. (USN)

(Below) A VAW-117 'Wallbangers' E-2C lines up behind a Jet Blast Deflector (JBD) before launching from NIMITZ (CVN-68). Its outer wings will unfold prior to launch. The E-2C has a distinctive 24 foot (7.3 M) diameter rotating radome and more than 12,000 pounds (5443 KG) of electronics. The Hawkeye can monitor six million cubic miles of airspace and more than 150,000 square miles of ocean surface. (USN by PH3 Yesenia Rosas)

NAVY 1, a Lockheed S-3B Viking from Sea Control Squadron Three Five (VS-35) 'Blue Wolves' successfully 'traps' (recovers) aboard USS ABRAHAM LINCOLN (CVN-72) on 1 May 2003. President George W. Bush – the first sitting President to trap aboard an aircraft carrier at sea – sat in the starboard seat for the flight. This Viking caught the Number 4 cable, or 'wire.' Bush's background as an Air National Guard F-102 pilot served him well on this flight. His political rivals dubbed this a 'stunt,' but this flight was a perfect reflection of a Commander-in-Chief who has shown remarkable leadership during a tough wartime era in American history. (USN by PHA Gabriel Piper)

(Right) President Bush passes through the 'side boys' after his successful landing aboard ABRAHAM LINCOLN, off the coast of San Diego, California. This Viking carried the call sign NAVY ONE during the flight while the President was aboard. The S-3B was originally developed primarily for Anti-Submarine Warfare (ASW). The Chief of Naval Operations deleted its ASW and Mine Warfare missions in December of 1999. ASW specific equipment was removed from the Navy's Vikings in Fiscal Year 2000 (FY00).

(Below Right) The President poses with sailors for a photo after his successful trap aboard ABRAHAM LINCOLN (CVN-72) in a VS-35 S-3B Viking designated 'NAVY 1.' Bush is the first sitting President to trap aboard an aircraft carrier at sea. The President visited the ship to meet with the sailors, then addressed the Nation as LINCOLN prepared to return from a ten-month deployment in support of Operation IRAQI FREEDOM. (USN by PH3 Tyler J. Clements)

(Below) A troubleshooter assigned to VS-35 'Blue Wolves' awaits the start of the next cycle of combat flight operations aboard ABRAHAM LINCOLN. He leans against a 'buddy store' air-refueling pod mounted under the S-3B's port wing. The high-endurance Vikings are used as tankers, transferring jet fuel to other aircraft. (USN by PH3 Philip A. McDaniel)

A VS-38 'Red Griffins' S-3B conducts routine missions from aboard USS CONSTELLATION (CV 64). Carrier Battle Group Commanders tasked the Vikings to provide surface surveillance and intelligence collection, electronic warfare, mine warfare, coordinated search and rescue, and fleet support missions, including air wing tanking. The sound of the S-3B's engines is often compared to that of a vacuum cleaner, hence its nickname, the 'Hoover.' (USN)

An S-3B Viking from VS-38 unfolds its wings before launching from CONSTELLATION. An F/A-18 Hornet assigned to another CVW-2 squadron is prepared for launching on the other waist catapult. (USN by PH3 Casey D. Tweedell)

An S-3B assigned to VS-21 'Red Tails' prepares to recover aboard KITTY HAWK (CV-63). The Viking's impressive surveillance capability consists of a sophisticated Electronic Surveillance Measures (ESM) suite and an Inverse-Synthetic Aperture Radar (ISAR). Both of these tools allow the S-3B to collect electronic intelligence invaluable to the battle group. Additionally, 'War Hoovers' have also been cleared to carry the AGM-84D Harpoon and AGM-65F Maverick missiles, giving the Viking an anti-surface capability to match its sensors. (USN by PH3 Todd Frantom)

A US Marine Corps (USMC) KC-130T loads cargo for resupply of Marine units fighting in Iraq. The aircraft is assigned to Marine Refueler Transport Squadron Four Fifty Two (VMGR-452), a Reserve unit based at Stewart International Airport (IAP), New York. Two aerial refueling basket pods mounted on the outboard wing undersurfaces enable this Hercules to refuel Marine and Navy aircraft in flight.

SSgt Jack Jassen directs a Sikorsky CH-53E Super Stallion to its parking spot near a C-130 Hercules. The helicopter brought Marines from an amphibious assault ship to a forward-deployed position during Operation IRAQI FREEDOM. The 386th Transient Alert Team played a key role in taking care of the aircraft transporting nearly 850 Marines moving forward to support operations in Iraq.

Marines of the 2nd Marine Expeditionary Brigade (MEB) walk on the flight deck of the WASP Class amphibious assault ship USS KEARSARGE (LHD-3). They flew back to the ship on CH-53Es after combat against Iraqi forces. KEARSARGE and the 2nd MEB were assigned to Amphibious Task Force – East (ATF-E) during IRAQI FREEDOM.

An F/A-18C Hornet returns from a combat mission over Iraq on 27 March 2003. This Hornet was assigned to Marine Fighter Attack Squadron One Fifteen (VMFA-115) 'Silver Eagles.' The Squadron flew with CVW-3 aboard USS HARRY S. TRUMAN (CVN-75) in the eastern Mediterranean Sea during the major combat phase in Iraq. Two AIM-9 Sidewinder Air-to-Air Missiles (AAMs) are mounted on the wingtips, while a 330 gallon (1249 L) fuel tank is mounted on the centerline rack. (USN)

(Above) An F/A-18C Hornet assigned to VMFA-232 'Red Devils' flies over Southwest Asia on 21 March 2003. It had just taken on fuel from a USAF KC-135 Stratotanker in the skies near Iraq. The Hornet is used as a fighter escort and fleet air defense; however, it can also be used as an attack aircraft with the capability of force projection, interdiction, as well as both close and deep air support. This dual capability gives commanders immense flexibility in wartime operations.

(Left) A Marine plane captain marshals a VMFA-251 'Thunderbolts' F/A-18C Hornet to a parking space at Al Jaber AB, Kuwait. The aircraft was later refueled and rearmed for its next mission. The 'Thunderbolts' were assigned to Carrier Air Wing Eight (CVW-8) aboard USS THEODORE ROOSEVELT (CVN-71) during Operation IRAQI FREEDOM. (USMC)

A Marine Tactical Electronic Warfare Squadron Two (VMAQ-2) EA-6B Prowler takes off from a forward deployed location on 22 March 2003. A pilot and one Electronic Countermeasures Officer (ECMO) sit in the forward cockpit, while two more ECMOs are in the aft cockpit. Gold imbedded in the canopies shields the crew from radiation emitted by the aircraft's Tactical Jamming System (TJS) pods. (USAF by SSgt Matthew Hannen)

(Right) A Boeing (McDonnell Douglas) AV-8B+ Harrier II makes a vertical landing aboard the amphibious assault ship USS BONHOMME RICHARD (LHD-6) after supporting Marine ground combat operations in southern Iraq. BONHOMME RICHARD and her embarked Harriers were in the Central Command Area of Responsibility (CENTCOM AOR) during Operation IRAQI FREEDOM. AV-8Bs made rolling take-offs from the assault ships to maximize its fuel reserves. (USN by PHAN Recruit Staci Bitzer)

(Below) Capt. Matthew, a Marine Attack Squadron Two Fourteen (VMA-214) 'Black Sheep' pilot, takes a careful walk around an AV-8B+ Harrier II during a pre-flight check on 12 April 2003. (His last name was withheld for security reasons.) VMA-214 is assigned to Marine Aircraft Group Thirteen (MAG-13) based at MCAS Yuma, Arizona. The 'Black Sheep' and their Harriers were deployed in support of Operation IRAQI FREEDOM. (USMC by Sgt Molly C. King)

A 1000 pound (454 KG) GBU-16 Paveway II Laser-Guided Bomb (LGB) is mounted on the port inboard wing station of this AV-8B. The LGB is decorated with a World Trade Center memorial sticker. A LANTIRN targeting pod was usually mounted on the Harrier's right inboard station. This combination of LGB and LANTIRN was a common load for USMC Harriers during Operation IRAQI FREEDOM. The Paveway II LGBs have folding aft wings, which replaced the fixed wings of earlier Paveway Is. The newer model also has an injection-molded plastic housing for the detector optics, which reduces both weight and cost. The detector has increased sensitivity for target detection. Paveway IIs also have reduced thermal battery delay after release, increased maximum canard (forward fin) deflection, laser coding, and an increased detector field of view. The Paveway II's laser detector has a 30 percent greater instantaneous field of view than on the earlier Paveway I.

An AV-8B+ Harrier II taxis to the ready position prior to launching from USS BATAAN (LHD-5) in the Persian Gulf on 23 March 2003. BATAAN hosted detachments from three Marine Harrier squadrons: VMA-223, VMA-231, and VMA-452. The latter unit subsequently deployed to Kuwait. The AV-8B+ features the AN/APG-65 radar fitted to the F/A-18 Hornet and other minor improvements, but is otherwise the same as earlier AV-8Bs. (USN by PH1 Jimmy D. Lee)

An AV-8B Harrier II pilot gets a 'fuels update' before taking off from BATAAN in the Persian Gulf on 18 March 2003. A deck crewman holds up a board showing the amount of fuel on board the aircraft. The AV-8B combines tactical mobility, responsiveness, reduced operating cost and basing flexibility, both afloat and ashore. They are particularly well-suited to the Marine Corps' special combat and expeditionary requirements. (USN by PH3 John Taucher)

Two VMFA-232 ordnance technicians, LCpl Adam Ingram (left) and Sgt Juan Jimenez, check a 500 pound (227 KG) GBU-12 LGB loaded onto an AV-8B's port inboard wing pylon. The operator – whether in the same aircraft, another aircraft, or on the ground – illuminates a target with a laser designator, then the munition guides to a spot of laser energy reflected from the target. The GBU-12 uses the standard 500 pound Mk 82 general purpose bomb. Aft of the weapons pylon is the lowered wing flap. (USMC by Sgt W.A. Napper, Jr.)

(Above) Cpl. Alvin Hicks, of Marine Wing Support Squadron 373's bulk fuels section, refuels a Bell AH-1W Super Cobra in a forward aircraft refueling point at Jalibah AB, Iraq on 22 March 2003. The Super Cobra is assigned to the Marine Light Attack Helicopter Squadron of the 3rd Marine Aircraft Wing (MAW), which is headquartered at MCAS El Toro, California. The Super Cobra is a day/night marginal weather USMC attack helicopter, which provides en route escort for assault helicopters and their embarked forces. It is the only Western attack helicopter with a proven air-to-air and anti-radar missile capability. The AH-1W's primary mission is as an armed tactical helicopter capable of close air support, low altitude and high speed flight, target search and acquisition, reconnaissance by fire, multiple weapons fire support, troop helicopter support, and point target attack of threatening armor. The Super Cobra provides fire support and fire support coordination to the landing force during amphibious assaults and subsequent operations ashore. It is armed with eight AGM-114 Hellfire anti-tank missiles on the stub wings and one 20MM M197 three barrel gun with 750 rounds under the nose. (USMC by LCpl Christopher H. Fitzgerald)

(Above Right) A CH-46D Sea Knight takes off with various members of the media bound for forward positions near Ad Diwanyah, Iraq on 30 March 2003. Typical field conditions – including sand, dust, and grass – created maintenance nightmares for aircraft mechanics. (USMC by LCpl Jennifer Krusen)

(Right) Task Force TARAWA headquarters was located at Blair Airfield, a captured Iraqi facility located at Al Kut, Iraq. Existing Hardened Aircraft Shelters (HASs) were retained to house Marine aircraft and heavy equipment. Vehicles and temporary storage facilities are located on and beside the taxiways leading to the HASs. (DOD by LCpl Bryan Nealy, USMC)

(Above) Two US Army Sikorsky UH-60 Black Hawk helicopters fly past the setting sun on 2 April 2003. They are flying to a forward-deployed location in southern Iraq during Operation IRAQI FREEDOM. (USAF by SSgt Shane A. Cuomo)

(Left) A UH-60A flies low over southern Iraq and its shadow during Operation IRAQI FREEDOM. The Black Hawk is the US Army's primary division-level transport helicopter, providing dramatic improvements in troop capacity and cargo lift capability compared to the Bell UH-1 Iroquois 'Huey' it replaces. The UH-60A has a crew of three and can lift an entire 11-man fully-equipped infantry squad in most weather conditions. It can be configured to carry four litters by removing eight troop seats in the Medical Evacuation (MEDEVAC) role. Both the pilot and co-pilot are provided with armor-protective seats. The UH-60's protective armor can withstand hits from 23MM shells. The Black Hawk has a cargo hook mounted on the centerline for external lift missions. It has provisions for mounting the M144 armament subsystem – consisting of two 7.62MM M60D machine guns – on the cargo doors. The helicopter can disperse chaff and infrared jamming flares using the M130 general purpose dispenser. The Black Hawk has a composite titanium and fiberglass four-bladed main rotor and its two 1622 SHP General Electric T700-GE-700 turboshaft engines give it a top speed of 163 MPH (132 knots/262 KMH).

Four UH-60s fly troops of the 2nd Brigade, 101st Airborne Division (Air Assault) over the outskirts of an unidentified Iraqi city on 5 April 2003. The 6th Battalion, 101st Aviation Regiment was the Black Hawks' parent organization within the Division, which deployed to the region from Fort Campbell, Kentucky. UH-60s were also assigned to the other Army divisions in Operation IRAQI FREEDOM. These units included the 1st Armored Division, 1st Infantry Division, 1st Cavalry Division, 3rd Infantry Division, 4th Infantry Division – Mechanized, the 82nd Airborne Division, and Task Force IRONHORSE. (US Army by Sgt Luis Lazzara)

This Boeing AH-64D Longbow Apache is parked at Tactical Assembly Area SHELL in central Iraq on 30 March 2003. It is assigned to Alpha Company, 2nd Battalion of the 101st Aviation Regiment. The AH-64D is a remanufactured and upgraded version AH-64A Apache. The primary modifications are the addition of a millimeter-wave Fire Control Radar (FCR) target acquisition system atop the rotor mast, the fire-and-forget Longbow AGM-114 Hellfire anti-tank missile, updated T700-GE-701C engines, and a fully-integrated cockpit. The AH-64D has improved survivability, communications, and navigation capabilities. (US Army by Sgt Igor Paustovski)

This AH-64D of A Company 2-101 crashed while landing at SHELL on 30 March 2003. In March of 2003, Iraqi anti-aircraft fire downed one Apache Longbow and damaged 14 others outside Baghdad. The Apaches were on a deep-attack mission, a dangerous mission that requires excellent intelligence, refueling sites, a rescue plan, and 'rally' points where crews can meet and successfully leave the area. The Iraqis were waiting for the Longbows and used cell phones to give advance notice to their troops, who were told: *"As soon as you hear them, fill the sky with lead."* Controversy later ensued over whether the costly Longbows – a high-tech version of the tank-killing Apache – were unnecessarily exposed to enemy fire on that mission. (US Army by Sgt Igor Paustovski)

CW2 Mark Borden sits in the cockpit of his AH-64D prior to taking off for a mission from SHELL on 30 March 2003. The Apache is armed with the 30MM M230 Automatic Gun, a single barrel, externally powered (3 HP electric motor), electrically fired, chain driven weapon. It is mounted in the lower section of the gun turret on the Apache's undersurface. The M230 fires a load of 1200 rounds of 30MM linkless ammunition at a rate of 625 shots per minute (SPM). The AH-64D is armed with eight AGM-114 Hellfire missiles on the stub wings. The AGM-114 is an anti-armor air-to-surface weapon, which uses a shaped charge warhead to defeat hard point targets with minimal exposure of the launch helicopter to enemy fire. The Hellfire Air-to-Ground Missile System (AGMS) provides heavy antiarmor capability for attack helicopters. (US Army by Sgt Igor Paustovski)

A Boeing Vertol CH-47D Chinook slings a large support trailer above the ground in central Iraq. The CH-47 is the US Army's workhorse and has served as the prime mover for the US Army and other military forces since 1960. Its principal missions include transport of troops, artillery, ammunition, fuel, water, barrier materials, supplies and equipment on the battlefield. By 1976, the Army signed a contract with Boeing to upgrade 472 CH-47A, B, and C model Chinooks into CH-47Ds.

While Operation IRAQI FREEDOM got all the headlines, Operation ENDURING FREEDOM continued to root out terrorists in Afghanistan. A CH-47D delivers troops of Bravo Company, 2/504th Infantry Regiment into the Baghni Valley of Afghanistan for participation in Operation VIPER on 1 March 2003. The Chinook can carry 38 fully-equipped troops or up to 26,000 pounds (11,794 KG) of cargo within its main cabin. (DOD by Sgt Vernall Hall)

Soldiers from A Company, 2nd Battalion, 327th Infantry Regiment, 101st Airborne Division (Air Assault) maintain Pick-up Zone posture on 4 May 2003. They were awaiting incoming UH-60 Black Hawk helicopters during Operation IRAQI FREEDOM. One UH-60 is parked alongside the road, while a truck with soldiers drives up to the area. (US Army by Spec Derek Gaines)

Members of the 1st Battalion, 82nd Aviation Regiment arrive in Bell OH-58D Kiowa Warrior helicopters for surveillance missions on 23 March 2003. The OH-58D is the US Army's fielded armed reconnaissance aircraft. The Kiowa Warrior is equipped with a Mast Mounted Sight (MMS) that includes a Television System, Thermal Imaging System, and a Laser Rangefinder/Designator. The helicopter also has an Embedded Global Positioning System (GPS) Inertial Navigation System (INS); airborne Target Handover System or Improved Data Modem for digital communication; HAVEQUICK II Ultra High Frequency (UHF) radios, two SINCGARS Frequency Modulation (FM) radios, and Very High Frequency (VHF) radio. The Kiowa has two Universal Weapons Pylons for mounting a total of two of the following weapons systems: AGM-114 Hellfire missiles, Raytheon AIM-92 Stinger air-to-air missiles, 2.75 inch (70MM) Hydra 70 rocket pods, and/or a .50 caliber (12.7MM) fixed machine gun. (USAF by SRA Tammy L. Grider)

(Below) A convoy of US Army and Air Force personnel enter the main entrance of an abandoned Iraqi Air Base to perform a sight-survey on 25 April 2003. They checked for booby traps and evaluated the facility for use by US and other Coalition units. Two Royal Air Force (RAF) Hercules aircraft are parked in the background. (USAF by SRA JoAnn S. Makinano)

(Below) A USAF Security Force member provides airfield security for the first civilian aircraft that landed at Baghdad International Airport (BIAP) on 24 April 2003. This aircraft brought in several International Committee of the Red Cross (ICRC) members and medical supplies. This made the ICRC the first Non-Governmental Organization (NGO) to arrive at BIAP since the commercial runway opened the day before. (USAF by SSgt Cherie A. Thurpoundy)

Three active Coalition members – the US, Great Britain, and Australia – are represented by these three servicemen. They are (left to right): MSgt Scott Tuttle, 379th Expeditionary Security Forces Squadron; Cpl Mark Jarvis, Royal Air Force Police; and Cpl Ben Pederson, Royal Australian Air Force Security Forces. Other large and small nations are publicly known to have contributed in some role to this Coalition of the Willing against Iraq. These nations include: Afghanistan, Albania, Angola, Azerbaijan, Bulgaria, Colombia, Costa Rica, the Czech Republic, Denmark, Dominican Republic, El Salvador, Eritrea, Estonia, Ethiopia, Georgia, Honduras, Hungary, Iceland, Italy, Japan, Kuwait, Latvia, Lithuania, Macedonia, Marshall Islands, Micronesia, Mongolia, the Netherlands, Nicaragua, Palau, Panama, the Philippines, Poland, Portugal, Romania, Rwanda, Singapore, Slovakia, Solomon Islands, South Korea, Spain, Tonga, Turkey, Uganda, Ukraine, and Uzbekistan. (USAF by SSgt David Donovan)

SADDAM...YOU ARE THE WEAKEST LINK "GOODBYE!!" is painted on the nose of an RAF Nimrod MR.1 deployed to the Persian Gulf. This parodies the line used to dismiss unsuccessful contestants on the TV game show "The Weakest Link." (RAF/Crown Copyright)

A shark mouth is painted on the nose of this BAE Systems Harrier GR.7 assigned to an unidentified RAF unit. Anti-Foreign Object Damage (FOD) covers are placed inside the engine intakes, while four 300 gallon (1136 L) fuel tanks are mounted on wing pylons. The RAF deployed their Harriers from bases in the United Kingdom (UK) to forward-deployed airfields in the Persian Gulf region.

A Tornado F.3 fighter from No. 111 (F) Squadron was named HAVE IT! A cartoon of Saddam Hussein seated in a MiG-29 fighter is hit in the forehead by a lightning bolt from the Squadron. (RAF/Crown Copyright)

(Right) A shark mouth and mission tallies are painted on the nose of this Panavia Tornado GR.4 deployed to Ali al Salem AB, Kuwait. The tallies under the windshield represent four bombing missions and nine attacks with BAE Systems Air-Launched Anti-Radiation Missiles (ALARMs). (RAF/Crown Copyright)

Rccts controller's dream and *The glory is in the giving* are painted with a Christmas tree on the nose of this Tornado GR.4. The British named their participation in the Iraq campaign Operation TELIC. (RAF/Crown Copyright)

(Below Right) A beaver rides a Laser-Guided Bomb (LGB) on B.A.B'S, another Tornado GR.4 deployed from Britain to Ali al Salem. Several mission tally markings are painted above the nose art. (RAF/Crown Copyright)

(Below) It's Show Time is painted on the nose of an RAF Tornado GR.4 deployed to the Persian Gulf. A scantily dressed woman sits astride a Storm Shadow stand-off weapon, which these Tornadoes employed in combat for the first time during Operation TELIC. (RAF/Crown Copyright)

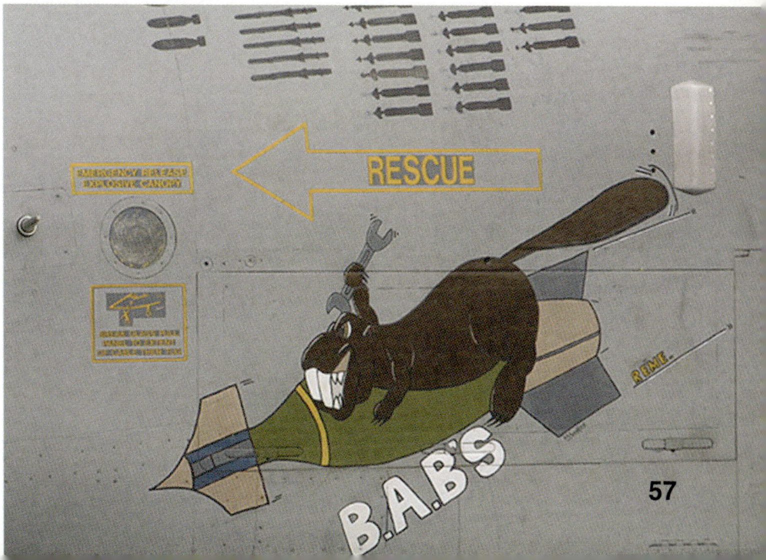

A No 3 Squadron pilot egresses from his Harrier GR.7 following a mission over Iraq. The aircraft's crew chief waits at the foot of the boarding ladder. The in-flight refueling probe is extended from the port engine intake cowling. Squadron pilots clocked up to 1000 flight hours during Operation TELIC. (RAF/Crown Copyright)

An RAF armorer prepares AGM-65 Maverick missiles before loading them aboard a Harrier GR.7. Harrier armament includes two 25mm ADEN cannon on under-fuselage stations. It can carry up to sixteen 500 pound (227 kg) Mk 82 or six 1000 pound (454 kg) Mk 83 bombs, or four Maverick air-to-surface missiles. Other weapons options include Paveway 2 and 3 LGBs, two AIM-9L Sidewinders or Advanced Short-Range Air-to-Air Missiles (ASRAAMs), Brimstone anti-armor missiles, CRV-7 rocket pods, or two Storm Shadow stand-off missiles on eight available wing stations.

The Harrier GR.7 is the RAF's primary Close Air Support (CAS) aircraft. It is capable of day and night operations and its Vertical and Short Take-Off and Landing (V/STOL) performance makes it an extremely flexible asset. The aircraft's Forward-Looking Infra-Red (FLIR) equipment combines with the pilot's Night Vision Goggles (NVGs) to provide a night, low level capability.

(Below) A Harrier GR.7 prepares for take-off in front of a Hardened Aircraft Shelter (HAS) in the Persian Gulf region. The Harrier GR.7 is essentially an AV-8B Harrier II fitted with RAF-specific navigation and defensive systems. The RAF version also has two additional underwing pylons for AIM-9 Sidewinder missiles. The Harrier GR.7's windshield is strengthened to resist birdstrikes in low level flight. This Harrier is armed with two Sidewinders and two 1000 pound (454 kg) LGBs.

A Tornado GR.4 crew – pilot and navigator/weapons officer – conduct preflight checks on a Storm Shadow stand-off missile. The Tornado-equipped No 617 Squadron debuted the Storm Shadow during Operation TELIC. The Matra BAe Dynamics Storm Shadow is an air-launched, conventionally-armed, precision weapon. It is deployable at night or day, in most weather and operational conditions, with a range of 155 miles (249 KM). Storm Shadow was developed to attack and destroy a wide variety of static, high value 'hardened' targets, including command and control facilities, airfield facilities, and bridges. (RAF/Crown Copyright)

(Right) An armorer removes the covers from a Matra BAe Dynamics ASRAAM before a Tornado F.3 sortie. ASRAAM is the world's first Infra-Red (IR) missile to enter service using a staring array detector, which detects the whole target 'scene.' The actual picture is highly similar to a monochrome TV picture, and gives the missile excellent long-range target acquisition capability and enhanced performance against any employed countermeasures. (RAF/Crown Copyright)

(Below) A Tornado GR.4, laden with two new Storm Shadow stand-off missiles, is prepared for a sortie from inside a HAS at Ali al Salem AB, Kuwait. The Tornado GR.4 is the result of a British Aerospace (now BAE Systems) upgrade for Tornado GR.1s, which added Forward-Looking Infra-Red (FLIR), a wide angle Head-Up Display (HUD), improved cockpit displays, and NVG compatibility. This latest variant also has new avionics and weapons systems, updated computer software, and Global Positioning System (GPS) receivers. The Tornado GR.4 upgrade also allows the aircraft to carry Storm Shadow missiles, Brimstone advanced anti-armor weapons, the Reconnaissance Airborne Pod for Tornado (RAPTOR) and Vicon reconnaissance pods, and the Thermal Imaging Airborne Laser Designator (TIALD) targeting pod. A separate program covered an integrated defensive aids suite consisting of the Radar Warning Receiver (RWR), Sky Shadow radar jamming pod, and BOZ-107 chaff and flare dispenser. (RAF/Crown Copyright)

Two RAF Tornado F.3s escort a USAF B-1B bomber as it refuels from a KC-10A. The Tornado F.3 is the RAF's primary air defense fighter. They are now equipped with the Joint Tactical Information Distribution System (JTIDS), which processes real time information on hostile aircraft obtained by sensors in other fighters or Airborne Early Warning (AEW) aircraft. The Tornado's crew can select its own target and move to within 'kill' distance without using the fighter's own search radar with its position-revealing signature until the last possible moment. (RAF/Crown Copyright)

Four RAF Vickers VC-10 K.3 tankers sit through a sandstorm alongside USAF KC-10A Extenders. These tankers were based at a forward-deployed location in CENTCOM's AOR. Sandstorms plagued the entire AOR early in Operation IRAQI FREEDOM/TELIC. (RAF/Crown Copyright)

Two Tornado F.3s refuel from a VC-10 K.3 tanker. The RAF deployed these tankers from Britain to the Persian Gulf region. Several F.3s were modified to carry the ALARM anti-radar missile as an urgent requirement for Operation TELIC. These aircraft were redesignated Tornado EF.3s. Eventually, these aircraft did not deploy to the Persian Gulf. The Tornado EF.3 is armed with two ALARMs on external pylons on the under-belly stations. These standard F.3s have four Skyflash air-to-air-missiles on the fuselage undersurface. (RAF/Crown Copyright)

The RAF deployed one of its seven Boeing Sentry AEW.1 (E-3D) aircraft to the AOR. The aircraft are flown by Nos 8 and 23 Squadrons at RAF Waddington, England and are the British contribution to the NATO Airborne Early Warning (AEW) Force. The Sentry's normal crew is 17, broken down into four flight deck crew, three technicians and a ten-man mission crew. The mission crew comprises a tactical director (mission crew commander), a fighter allocator (director), two weapons controllers, a surveillance controller, two surveillance operators, a data manager, a communications operator and an electronic support measures operator. (RAF/Crown Copyright)

Personnel of No 617 Squadron – the famous 'Dambusters' – celebrate the 60th anniversary of their formation on and under one of their Tornado GR.4s at Ali al Salem. Three red lightning bolts are painted on the Tornado's tail, while 1943 and 2003 are located on the lower vertical tail. No 617 Squadron is possibly the most famous RAF squadron currently flying. It was formed at RAF Scampton, England on 21 March 1943 specifically to undertake Operation CHASTISE – the breaching of dams vital to the German war effort. This mission was successfully undertaken on the evening of 16/17 May 1943. The movie "The Dambusters" was based on this mission. (RAF/Crown Copyright)

RAF SEPECAT Jaguar GR.3As deployed from RAF Coltishall, England to Turkey for Operation TELIC. The Jaguar is capable of employing 1000 pound (454 KG) retard and free fall bombs, CBU-87 cluster munitions, Paveway 2 and 3 LGBs, CRV-7 rocket pods, and two 30MM ADEN cannon. Two AIM-9L Sidewinder air-to-air missiles are mounted on overwing hardpoints for self-defense. The Jaguar can be fitted with a 317 gallon (1200 L) external fuel tank on the centerline pylon, or two tanks under the wings. In the reconnaissance role, it can utilize conventional 'wet film' and Electro-Optical (EO) sensors in an external pod. It can also carry the Thermal Imaging Airborne Laser Designator (TIALD) pod for self-designation or co-operative designation of precision-guided weapons. Self-defense systems include Skyguardian RWR, an AN/ALQ-101-10 (V) Electronic Countermeasures (ECM) pod, a Phimat chaff pod, and ALE-40 chaff and flare dispensers. (RAF/Crown Copyright)

A BAe Nimrod MR.2 takes off from Thumrait, Oman on an Operation TELIC mission over the Persian Gulf. This aircraft deployed from its home at RAF Kinloss, Scotland for the conflict. Nimrods fly Anti-Submarine Warfare (ASW), Anti-Surface Unit Warfare (ASUW), and Search and Rescue (SAR) missions. This aircraft has an unrefueled endurance of approximately ten hours.

An RAF Chinook HC.2 is parked at a forward-deployed location, while a Royal Navy (RN) Westland Sea King HC.2 lifts off. The British Chinooks – similar to the US Army's CH-47Ds – deployed from RAF Odiham, England.

(Below) Britain's Army Air Corps deployed Westland Lynx AH.7s to the CENTCOM AOR for Operation TELIC. The Lynx's primary role is as an anti-tank helicopter. It carries eight AGM-71 TOW (Tube-Launched, Optically-Sighted, Wire-Guided) Anti-Tank Guided Missiles (ATGMs) and is equipped with a stabilized roof sight with dual (day and night) magnification.

(Above) An Aérospatiale/Westland SA-330J Puma operated by civilian contractor Geo-Seis Helicopters gets the lift-off signal on the flight deck of USS HARRY S. TRUMAN (CVN-75) in the eastern Mediterranean. Similar British Army Puma HC.2s supported patrols and carried out casualty evacuation flights during Operation TELIC. (USN by PHA Ryan O'Connor)

An RAF Canberra PR.9 is prepared for a reconnaissance mission during Operation TELIC. The original English Electric Canberra design dates from the 1940s and the prototype first flew in 1949. The type first entered RAF operational service as a medium bomber in 1951. Short Brothers in Belfast, Northern Ireland built 23 Canberra PR.9s under license between 1958 and 1962.

A Royal Australian Air Force (RAAF) F/A-18A Hornet refuels from an USAF KC-135 over international waters south of Basra, Iraq during a combat mission over Iraq on 7 April 2003. The RAAF deployed 14 F/A-18s from No 75 Squadron at RAAF Tindal, Northern Territories to Kuwait. (RAAF)

An RAAF F/A-18 pilot checks a wing-mounted 500 pound (227 KG) GBU-12 LGB prior to an Operation FALCONER mission. The cockpit access ladder is extended from its position in the port Leading Edge Extension (LEX). Australia's Hornets fly both air defense and ground attack missions.

Two Australian Army CH-47D Chinooks fly troops and equipment over western Iraq on 22 April 2003. The Australians deployed three CH-47Ds from the 5th Aviation Regiment at Townsville, Queensland to Kuwait for Operation FALCONER – Australia's name for their role in Operation IRAQI FREEDOM. Australian Chinooks primarily flew in support of Australia's Special Forces Task Group.

Two Kuwaiti Air Force (KAF) F/A-18C Hornets refuel at the hot refuel pit at Ali al Salem AB, Kuwait on 22 April 2003. The aircraft are refueled while their engines keep running, which allows for faster turnaround time between missions. The Kuwaitis shared this base with USMC F/A-18s during Operation IRAQI FREEDOM. The *al-Quwwat al-Jawwiya al-Kuwaitiya* (Kuwait Air Force) received 32 F/A-18Cs and eight two-seat F/A-18Ds between January of 1992 and August of 1993. (USMC by Sgt W. A. Napper, Jr.)

An RAAF F/A-18A Hornet waits to refuel from an USAF KC-135 high over international waters south of Basra, Iraq during a combat mission on 7 April 2003. This Hornet carries AIM-9 Sidewinders on the wingtips, 1000 pound (454 KG) LGBs and 330 gallon (1249 L) fuel tanks under the wings, and another tank on the centerline. Two VFA-27 F/A-18Cs from USS KITTY HAWK (CV-63) fly near their Australian colleague.

The nose cone and cockpit canopy are open on *Persian Princess*, a Canberra PR.9 in the AOR. The navigator entered the aircraft through the open nose cone. This Canberra deployed to the Persian Gulf region from No 39 Squadron at RAF Marham, England. An Iraqi flag and nine mission tally marks are painted under the cockpit.

PFC Randall Rieves, a VMFA (AW)-121 plane captain, refuels a KAF F/A-18C at Ali al Salam's hot refuel pit on 22 April 2003. The Marines' operational tempo prevented the Kuwaitis from using this pit for their own Hornets until that day. AIM-9 Sidewinders are mounted on the Hornet's wingtips, while AGM-88 HARM anti-radiation missiles are loaded on the outboard wing pylons. (USMC by Sgt W. A. Napper, Jr.)